**ANCHOR**
BOOKS

DESTINATION SOMEWHERE

Edited by

Sarah Marshall

First published in Great Britain in 2004 by
ANCHOR BOOKS
Remus House,
Coltsfoot Drive,
Peterborough, PE2 9JX
Telephone (01733) 898102

SB ISBN 1 84418 295 9

FOREWORD

Anchor Books is a small press, established in 1992, with the aim of promoting readable poetry to as wide an audience as possible.

We hope to establish an outlet for writers of poetry who may have struggled to see their work in print.

The poems presented here have been selected from many entries, and as always editing proved to be a difficult task.

I trust this selection will delight and please the authors and all those who enjoy reading poetry.

Sarah Marshall
Editor

CONTENTS

Rainbow!

I see a rainbow, way up high,
Stretching across the cloudy sky,
With colours of beauty glowing through,
To capture this beauty, and wrap around you.

Like a coat made of colours, by Heaven above,
Wrapping this coat that is made full of love,
To make you feel joyful, happy and glee,
To never be sad, be loving and free.

But trying to catch this rainbow above,
Would take an eternity, of harmonious love,
The love that we need to get on with our lives,
To forever stay happy, with the will to survive.

Janet Brook

WHEN DARKNESS FALLS HE RULES

He slumbers till the day grows old
One with stripes and black and gold
Sleeping there until the night
Preparing for the next long fight
When darkness falls he rules

As it comes to end of day
Time to awake and find some prey
With eyes that glisten in the night
Seeing all with feline sight
When darkness falls he rules

Stalking through the undergrowth
Is that a snake or a sloth?
He listens with a well-pricked ear
And all around the sound is fear
When darkness falls he rules

He looks up and smells the air
Now he senses something there
Crouching low and out of sight
He wants his prey to stay and fight
When darkness falls he rules

No sorrow or remorse does he feel?
To him it's only another good meal
When he's had his fill and the eating is done
He'll leave for scavengers' skin and bone
When darkness falls he rules

He slumbers till the day grows old
One with stripes of black and gold
Sleeping there until the night
Preparing for the next long fight
When darkness falls he rules.

Steven Frederick Burns

SIGH AND STORM

Thousand waves rose in ocean,
Thousand waves kissed the shore,
Thousand waves were then gone,
And my heart all bore.

Fiercely the tempest grew,
Madly the tide leaped,
Terribly the nor'west blew,
And calmly I peeped.

But I fear if my tear
Burst the barrier of my beach.
Let my pain die and wane,
Shall it then never you reach.

A single ripple in thy lake,
And a single heavy sigh of thine,
All my composure deeply shake
And madden waves of mine.

Asaduzzaman Malik

To Work Or Bus(t)

Waiting for that bus to arrive watching life go by
I often wonder if it's worth the wait
To stand here and comply
The cars whiz past in their comfortable glee
Driving to the beat
I'm standing in this line of citizens
A bus they'd like to meet

While waiting for this red conveyer
There are thoughts loves gone by
What happened to that Brenda girl?
It's something I'll wonder why
We seemed to blend so easily
Together we were one
She started those maternal feelings
Aha . . . problem's just begun.

Sophia was an odd one, with thoughts to save the planet
Amazon forest, panda bears
Not natural, she will ban it
Marcia was a Pisces a believer in her stars
She believed we'd all die in two weeks
I think she's now living on Mars.

I see a man a-running, running towards me quickly
The bus is on the horizon
And I think it's my No 50
People shuffle forward not to lose their place in line
Showing their passes with contempt
Their long wait is felt a crime.

As people scramble forward to the sardine tin on wheels
Space is running out to board
And it's no more driver feels
Rejected from the packed out tin, long wait beholds me now
Standing at the stop along
To walk is now my vow.

Steve Beckles-Ebusa

THE UNFORTUNATE VOLUNTEER

I'll tell you of the time I was hypnotised
as fingers snapped and clicked till I was mesmerised,
with eagerness I volunteered excited as can be
but things didn't go too well - as you will soon but see.
We all sat in a circle, and clasped each others' hand
when tapped upon the shoulder, up we'd get and stand.
I've always liked a laugh, or maybe even two
but it isn't very funny - when they poke the fun at you!
With eyes now tightly shut, I was put in a deep trance
tapped upon the shoulder, and told to ballet dance.
So clumsily I took the stage, and tried to do the splits
as the audience keeled over, uncontrollably in fits!
I pranced about on tippy toes, thinking I looked cool
but what was to happen next, made me look an utter fool.
The band now started playing music to Swan Lake!
As I danced now with my partner, my legs began to ache.
I was swung in all directions, and spun around too fast
then slipped and lost my balance, as the audience looked aghast.
I tumbled off the stage and fell into 'The Band',
the hypnotist raced over and tried to keep 'the upper hand!'
Quickly I was rushed, with a bump upon the head
to the accident and emergency, where I spent a week in bed.
I was rather black and blue, with bruises now galore
and bandaged like a mummy, I didn't half feel sore!
My evening had ended, not as I had planned
I had a golf ball on my head, and a badly broken hand!
I felt I'd lost all dignity, and felt humiliation -
I was certainly going to strive, for a lot of compensation!
I did try to see the funny side, as this was really weird
but I really have myself to blame -
cos I went and volunteered!

Alison Lambert

PLEASE COME TO DINNER

We sailed across the Spanish main
Cut off their head and ate their brain,
We boil the head in a great pot
And ate the brawn when it was still hot.
We tear the rib cage wide apart
And took out the still warm heart.
On the fire that heart we roast
Drink some wine as a grand toast.
Toss their bodies into a nearby river
Minus of course, their kidneys and liver,
It's very tender if they're still young
We find it hard to cook their tongues.

The chef I've said let's make meat pies
I will make the gravy with their eyes.
We will have to soak the meat
Tender on the leg, hard on the feet.
We scrape the bones from shoulder and hip
Make bait for the fish out of the lip.
Dry out the lung to make a sheath
Made tools out of the nails and teeth,
We made bricks from the local mud
Mix it with the pot of fresh blood.
Across the island our food did smell
You can never say we did not eat that well.

Colin Allsop

SAINTS AND HEROES

Saints and heroes; to me they're the same,
Salt of the earth who always play the game;
Saints, unobtrusively, behind the scenes,
Helping wherever by whatever means.

We all know some saints; they give of their best,
Never failing to respond when put to the test.
They give their time, talents, love, their all,
Always there to help when our backs are to the wall.

Heroism's a spur of the moment thing.
Out of the blue the hero's ready to spring
Into action, influenced by events,
Not stopping to think or becoming too tense.

For speed's of the essence, there's a life to save,
And so this person, undoubtedly brave,
Metaphorically speaking, jumps in the deep end;
It could be anyone moved by the event.

Heroes aren't always big, strong and vigilant;
Think of David who slew Goliath the giant.
So to me saints and heroes are one and the same,
The selfless who seek neither fortune nor fame.

Marlene Allen

GOLDEN LEAVES

I have not experienced,
such an awesome thrill,
as sitting under a tree of gold,
high on a hill . . .

Soon the winds began to blow, and
branches swayed to and fro . . .

Golden leaves blowing away . . .
Swirling, and twirling . . .
Golden leaves in the air . . .
I looked up to find, leaves
no longer there . . .
The tree on the hill was suddenly bare . . .

I got so caught up in this autumn day . . .
I felt like a child, having fun at play.

Carol Olson

UNTITLED

Sorry I missed your birthday
I really am a clown
But this month in general was
Turned almost upside-down.

Did the local postman come
Knocking at your door?
I hope you had a grand day
Cards, gifts and so much more.

I trust you dined and did
The town to celebrate
Sorry I missed your birthday
So this card is somewhat late.

You must reveal your age sometime
For I am in the dark
Be sure to make a fuss next year
And really make your mark.

Jacky Edwards

OBSERVING THE CUSTOMERS

I stand at the door at a minute to eight
And watch all the customers as they wait
They look at me frantic as if in a race
So I just look back with a smile on my face
The one at the front has her trolley held tight
Gripping the handles her knuckles are white
I walk to the door and turning the key
Faces light up, do you think it's for me?
The doors they are open and in they all run
Watching them looks to me like it is fun
Off goes the first one, produce to get
She passes the cabbage, but has Swede instead
Over to Weetabix, jam, marmalade
You'd think up her rear they had shoved a grenade
Straight down the next isle, without a fuss
She has to get finished, but will never rush
Hands on the soup tins, tomato will do
Pasta and rice, baked beans, Irish stew
Down to the bottom to pick up her mags
And on the way out I suspect she'll have fags
She's first at the check-out, on till number two
With a brief little chat and a quick 'toodaloo'
She's out of the door now as quick as she came
Pension I guess, 'cause it's Monday again.

Patricia H Moore

PORTRAIT OF A POET

Famous Seamus and the humble spud,
'Squelch and slap' of ignoble mud,
Pity and fear, when only six,
Pro-life, for 'scraggy wee s**ts'
Later, feigning callousness
'Bloody pups' a rural mess.

Book-learning was his great escape,
The first-born, blessed with fame at last,
Picking the scab that is the past,
Outlived Larkin, he dwells in marble halls,
Life-size, freely-brushed, in foggy winter hues,
Far from dirt-poor rural turf,
He lives in books, but hangs on walls.

Bill Looker

BIG ISSUE, BIG ISSUE

'Big Issue, Big Issue' they all walk past
He just trying to make a few bob so he doesn't have to fast.
He's obviously homeless people do say,
An alkie or junkie, it's not always the way.
He does not want hand outs pity or ****,
Just a place to sleep not another hit.

'Big Issue, Big Issue,' but still no joy.
'Look Mum, look Mum look at that boy,'
The words can be cruel, the stares they can hurt,
'Yes I am homeless with a badge on my shirt,'
A picture a number a badge of my own,
Come on now, it's no compensation for a family home.

'Big Issue, Big Issue,' a punter has come,
'What's wrong Son, where is your Mum?'
I am not an alkie or junkie oh no!
My parents both died I had nowhere to go.
I've been through the system but people don't care
Was raped and abused, hence the lonely stare.
I just want help, I just want hope.
I just want a friend to help me cope.

'Big Issue, Big Issue,' I am going to bed,
Just over there in the garden shed.
Another day over, another will arise
But I have no dreams to dream when I close my eyes.

Craig Boyd

HEATWAVE 2

I've had quite enough of this heatwave,
I wish it would all go away,
Nothing but glorious sunshine,
Repeatedly, day, after day.

It's nice to go out without coats on,
Better still, to stay in, in the cool,
And as for the thought of sunbathing,
How can anyone be such a fool?

Maybe, when it's constantly raining,
I'll think of these days with regret,
But somehow, I don't really think so,
Quite frankly, I'd rather get wet.

Wilma Morris

THE FRARK

The Frark is an animal who lives in an ark.
His terrible bite is worse than his bark.
Upon his hind legs he stands ten feet tall.
He chews all the paper off the living room wall.
He chews all the paper and swallows the paste,
but won't eat the flowers because of the taste.
He jumps out the window and runs up the road,
and sometimes has glimpses of turkey and toad.
When foggy he can get no breakfast at all,
for turkey is murky and toad in the hole.
He also likes cornflakes and sometimes friend mole,
but if he can't get them he just eats the bowl.

Anthony Kent

BONFIRE NIGHT

The darkness of the night
Lit up with light
Of a million stars
That shine so bright
Floating through the sky
Then fall to Earth
And vanish out of sight.

So many colours to be seen
Different noises as they scream
So much to see and hear in the night
Fears and excitement for the kids delight
All this done by a strike of a light
Money turned to ashes for Bonfire Night.

Elizabeth Harris

THE BEST MEDICINE

Did you know it is really true? What most people say
Laughter is the best medicine, and we should use some every day.

The world at the moment, is full of trouble and strife,
But if we learn to laugh, it will brighten up our life.

Laughing is really good, it's a source of letting go!
And it's also very contagious, when it's in full flow.

When you've mastered a giggle, or a little snigger,
Try a laugh from your belly, full of joy and vigour.

Laughing is very good, it clears the lungs and gives you a lift,
It's installed in every one of us, a beautiful expressive gift.

Everyone should try and laugh, and get on with each other,
Then we'd see more neighbourly love, love of man and brother.

So when you can laugh out loud, and can be happy with yourself,
It won't take very long, to see an improvement in your health.

Karon Crocombe

My Puppy

He loves to bark at the cows and calves,
But he hates having baths.
He loves eating food,
But he's not always good.

He pulls on the lead,
And you would never believe his speed.
He likes to chase my cat,
And always will sit for a wee pat.

He loves to be tickled under the chin,
And tries to eat from the rubbish bin.
Rolly I love you,
Yes I do.

Sarah Banks

NEVER

I never say I love you
I never say I care
But all my thoughts are with you
Whenever you're not there.

I never tell you how I feel
Whenever we're apart
Because you're always with me
Deep within my heart.

I never walk a street alone
Though you're not there to see
You'll always be within my mind
Ever close to me.

Whether together or far apart
You know, my love, you have my heart
You have my heart till time stands still
And that my love, it never will.

James Johnston

WHAT I SAW

I did not see what I saw
I didn't even see it.
But if I saw what I'd seen
I'd tell you, but would you believe it?

If you saw what I'd seen
Would you tell me that you saw it?
Then you know that what I saw
Was both what we saw, cos we have seen it.

Niall McManus

In God She Believes
(Dedicated to my sister Liz)

The sky is grey and dark
A storm is brewing
The water is surging and foaming
Breaking into high waves
Although they come close
They don't touch her - nothing touches
The sand she walks is dry
Trudging along mind in turmoil
She steps away from the water's edge
Her spirit tries to understand
Why she feels so alone - downhearted!
Suddenly the fog rises - morning dawns
She watches the sun rise - a new day
Looking back to yesterday
She knows she won't walk that path again
She endured for the sake of her spirit
Her immortal soul knew -
She had lost interest in human life!
It abandoned her earthly body
And flies towards the light -
In God she believes.

Moira McAllister Brown

ODE TO OLD POPS

Of bairns he was one of eleven
Four sisters and six brothers he was given
He left school early in a bothy he did stay
And worked hard on the farms by night and by day.

To follow the plough with horse was his choice
Two great Clydesdales would obey only his voice
He met and married a lassie named Lizzie
And for some years they just kept themselves busy
Working on the farms and out in the fields
Till one March day a son she did yield.

Proud father and mother of son number one
Five years later another came along
They nurtured and loved their family of two
Then the sons flew the nest to take wives, as they do.

So along came five grandchildren all different in many ways
Old Grandad would look after his grandkids
After work on school days
And now three great grandchildren has old pops
They live in a wee house now, but he never stops
He's out in his garden or away on the bus
So let's raise a glass dear dad just to say
Thank you from all of us.

Annie Mac

So Old

My teacher is so old he used to communicate
     using smoke signals, carrier pigeons and Morse code.
My teacher's so old he thinks a CD is a spelling
     of 'seedy' - like a potato that's ready to plant.
He thinks a floppy disk is an old record that won't play properly.
He thinks a 'hard drive' is a long journey on a motorway at night.
He thinks 'voice mail' is when you phone up to complain
                    to a newspaper.
He thinks 'IT' is a game he used to play in the playground.
My teacher's so old that he's even older than my dad!

Chris Lawrence-Jones

PRISONERS OF WAR 1940

We fought to the last held our grand made our stand, now
my comrades lay dead in this sodden cursed land.

I called out in anguish Lord! Where is thy light, all
around me was darkness my day was my night.

In my mind where the screams I had heard and the noise
I covered my ears tried to drown out their cries.

I was blind, in despair, afraid to move on, then I heard
a voice saying, 'Come on lad time we were gone.'

He took told of my arm 'Through my eyes you will see
I'll guide you old son just you hold on to me.'

Together we stumbled and walked side by side, his voice
sad but strong was tinged with strange pride.

Many comrades were murdered under a white flag of truce
the cold butcher's bayonet was used with abuse.

Men surrounded with honour and died where they stood the
hands of 'the butchers' were stained with their blood.

For thousands were captured, and yet thousands more
escaped to the beaches and as they left the shore.

They vowed to return, they could never forget
for they would remember (this black day *was* met)

By an army so strong in its anger and pride,
they would come as avengers, the Lord would abide.

But now Dunkirk had fallen, Calais and the Somme,
many thousands were captured, many thousands fought on.

As we stumbled for miles in the filth and grime
my thoughts kept repeating, vengeance is mine.

Though our bodies were battered, our spirit was strong
men's voices were singing, and then all along.

More voices were rising, their songs filled the air
God's light had shone through, He had answered my prayer.

Many years would pass by, but this war would be won
this evil would perish God's Will Be Done.

June Pledger

SMALL COG

I worry and rush to catch the train
I sometimes walk, miserable task in the rain,
In the sun I cannot hurry
The air is too still,
I have to be there early
Which takes all my will.
I must get to the meeting
To give my voice
So the people I speak for
Have a choice
This to me is vital
The networking of information.
I am only a small cog,
But there are many across the nation.
One day people will change,
And look beyond what they see,
When they meet a mental case
When they meet me.

Pauline Stevens

I'M JUST ME

My happiness is you,
But why should I be happy?
I'm no one special, I'm just me.
I'm here to love, not be loved,
I'm here to give not to receive,
My life is my family,
My family are my life.
Why should I be different?
I should be glad I can love,
What makes me feel the way I do?
Which life is me loving,
Or being loved,
Why can't I have both?
I can't because
I'm no one special
I'm just me!

L M Randell

HUNTED

A claw as sharp and hand held tight
Stalking tigress and lady walk
Darkening jungle and dim-lit street
Strong tiger and manly figure they meet.
The tiger's eye, the manly stare
Slinking shoulders, held out chest
Stiffened pose, hypnotic gaze
Jungle nights and lazy days
Two that prowl and two that walk
His sabre fangs, his knowing smile
Behind as one, as two embrace
Roaring purrs and pulses race
Her playful snarl, her deepened breath
Secluded bush and lovers room
The final roar, last uttered cry
Two tigers part, two bodies, weakened lie.

Nicola Jayne Green

EATING WORMS

The little lad was chewing on a worm in his back yard,
'Don't eat worms our Alfred,' said his mother and hit him very hard.
'His mommy will be looking for him,' her voice was fit to burst,
'She won't be looking for his mommy because I ate her first.'

Don Goodwin

MURPHY'S OUTING

Three drunk men came rolling in
One was fat and one was thin
The other was a snotty sod
He wouldn't carry Murphy's hod.

He knew he made the gaffa mad
With that barrow thing, it was bad
Murphy's legs were still in plaster
And those crutches he couldn't master.

Now Murphy's arm still in the sling
Just would not hold anything
And so he's had to drop the hod
Right onto the snotty sod.

Snotty has gone really barmy
Fatty said, 'Let him join the Army.'
Skinny said, 'He is such a dope
There ain't an army that could cope.'

Murphy tripped Fatty with the crutch
He said, 'That didn't hurt too much.'
He will be better by next day
Because it's time to get their pay.

Murphy is rather a stupid clot
And sometimes seems to lose the plot
He shoved old Snotty on his arse
And really hurt his kyber pass.

Fatty and Skinny have to agree
He's not going to take much more from he
Murphy's batting a sticky wicket
This really isn't playing cricket.

If it was, old Murphy says
I'd put a ball straight in his face
Skinny says, 'Well I ain't game
This is anything but tame.

So have another pint or four
Before you knock him on the floor
Remember he is taking you home
He told you that on the phone.

If you want him to load your bricks
Don't get up to anymore tricks
So let's all leave the pub right now
We can't stand up anyhow!'

Pauline A E Marshall

A Terrible Storm

Dark clouds are racing across the sky,
Meeting the horizon, and then starting to cry,
The rains pour down, and may make a flood,
Causing damage, and injury, and the spilling of blood,
The clouds are getting darker and making a deep rumbling sound,
And the flashing of lightning that is searing the ground,
The thunder is crescending to a terrible roar,
The sky is lit up just like a war,
The people and skyline is silhouetted in black.
Let's hope this storm breaks soon and not to come back.
The children are scared as they race for home,
Getting wetter and wetter and soaked to the bone,
The streets are like river, cascading its course,
What's left in its path, will be carried by force,
When the storm abates we will be counting the cost,
Of what Mother Nature has unleashed and what we have lost.

D Cole

Ease - Please

Quaking choking - endless smoking
There is no joking - you are taxed
Always trembling - seems never ending
Have you that dealer faxed
Now in trouble - sink another 'double'
Do you feel stressed and out of sorts?
As bills you fumble - near take a tumble
Dread the possibility of appearances in courts
Wish for some ease - work you could cease
To have more time for wife and kids
Listen to this please - uncross your knees
On those 'boiling pots' - put their lids
Find some space to still those fears
Untie tight girth find your real worth
Have some thought for your late years
The human race is - fact to face is
There is limited time to spend on earth
Some things evil - if you the hours fill
You'll find trouble - bent up double
Face up now to ease those backs
Untie those knots don't your life tax
Give some thought to now you ought to
Find the time to now relax!

Jon El Wright

SOMEONE

You could do with someone to share your life,
At my age, I don't need any trouble and strife,
'Go get a puppy dog' was the stern remark,
So I did and she came with female marks,
Maxi? But that's a dog's name
Never mind, she never puts me to shame,
At the pond, canal, she's at her best on the river,
She raises a laugh with anglers as we watch the quiver,
I sit and look at her, and think *where would I be?*
Some dingy bar drowning my sorrows?
Nope! We are off to the River Trent tomorrow!

Andrew I B Vaughan

THE SOLUTION

When things go wrong, and you can't cope
Searching for a miracle, to give you hope
To wake in the morning, to a wonderful day
Trusting, that at last, you will find a way.

A good breakfast, to tide you over
Looking, for that wonderful, field of clover
A cheery smile, from a passer by
Makes you feel better, give it a try.

The daily chores, you have to complete,
So take care of yourself, give life a treat.
Dispense with that miserable frown
Smile and the sun makes everything wear a crown.

Open your gate, with a confident air
A spring in your step, to show you care
Head, held high and a will to survive
To show the world, you are still alive.

All the worry, from days of yore
Seem to vanish and are no more.
Be determined to smile and be happy instead
For all the days that are now ahead.

C King

YOU AND I

You have the most gorgeous green eyes,
They twinkle and sparkle all the while,
They turn me on like a flashing green gem,
You're my best friend and my lover,
My wonderful Ben.

People say we are good together you and I,
We feed off each other like the spider and the fly,
We've done well together through laughter and tears,
Our love growing stronger through the passing of years.

We'll grow old together you and I,
And keep saying hello! And not goodbye.

Cheryl Campbell

I'D LIKE TO BE THERE

I'd like to be there on my funeral day,
To see what they wear and hear what they say.
I'd listen intently (unseen of course!)
And thank them for coming until I was hoarse.
I'd sit in a pew as the mourners went by,
And sing all the hymns, but try not to cry.
And then when they lowered me into the earth,
I'd lift up the lid and chuckle with mirth!

Margaret Bottomley

THE FLOWER STORY

I started out as a seed,
And grew and grew and grew,
When I reached the soil,
That was when I knew,
I'd soon be big and strong,
Just like all of you.

A few days later,
I grew some more,
Which made me realise,
I was not a seed anymore!
All of my friends,
Were really amazed,
At my big yellow petals,
And my leaves waxy glaze.

I grew and grew and grew some more,
And everyone knew I was so very tall,
I reached the clouds,
And touched the sky,
The sun then went and said goodbye.

After which I was no longer tall,
My petals dropped off by the wind an' all,
I decided to go back to being a seed,
And maybe I'll come back,
Early next spring.

Julia McAllister

PASSING TIME

Clouds drift across the sky in
different shapes and forms.
The sun sheds forth its rays of light
so beautiful and warm.
A harp is played, so gently comforting
and light, thoughts of bygone days
    makes imagination take flight.

The gentle waters of the lake lap
against the shore, cool breezes
kiss the sun warmed face and calm
returns once more.
Forget your troubles for a while,
enjoy the peace and calm, for life
is full of cares and stress and we
need time to refresh and be calm.

Walk along the lakeside, sit awhile
and think! Of all life has bestowed on you
and where life's gone in a wink.
Childhood memories come flooding back,
the dreams and ambitions you had.
Rekindle the flame of your carefree youth
as you try to recapture the same.

But the years, *alas*! are gone, so while in
the autumn of your years those wistful
thoughts still linger on, we can still
dream of what could have been,
        even though time has gone!

Gwyneth Llewellyn Rea

EASTER

Easter is the start of spring
When all the birds start to sing
The lambs are all being born
And the bears are starting to yawn
All the flowers start to grow
While all the bad weather starts to go
Chicks are clucking all around
Making such a funny sound
All the flowers are being bundled
While chocolate eggs are being munched
Butterflies are fluttering by
In the spring sky
That's what Easter's all about.

Rebecca Bamford

Holiday

A little work, a little rest
A little pleasure of the best.
A little cash to wisely spend
A kindly word for every friend.

The simple pleasures of the mind
Are here for all who wish to find.
Much beauty dwells on every land
On lake, on fell and meadowland.
Let every heart its tribute raise
In thankfulness itself in praise.

D Douglas

THE THIRD LANE

In his metal box he sat
His all enclosing
All protective box.
A distinctive colour, midnight black
The salesman had told him that.

Very proud, almost a bore
Just listen to that engine roar
Stops on a pinhead
Who needs more.
A safety car the makers say
Saint Christopher has had his day.

Carefully he'd run her in
And now out for his first real spin
He straddled the crown
His foot hard down
And swept by all
But suddenly that dot ahead was not so small.

The crazy fool he dryly mouthed
Can he not identify
The piece of road I occupy?
But he'll give way (they always do)
This time his opponent thought that too!

A grinding, tearing, ripping mesh
Mangled metal, human flesh
His safety car's no more
But he is safe for ever and again
If dying really was his final aim.

John Cooper

YOUR PRESENCE

We feel your presence all around
Watching over us without a sound
Like a twinkle in our eye
As the stars shine brightly in the sky
Flying free with the angels near
A calm feeling without any fear
As calm as the breeze on a summer's day
That guides the sailors
On their way.

Maria Jayne Halliday

CHILDHOOD MEMORIES

Strawberry jam on hot buttered toast,
This is the tea that I loved the most.
In a room lit with firelight, softly aglow.
Whilst out of the window, all is white with the snow.

Trees so tall they reach up to the sky,
My never-ending questions, of why oh why.
Why is Dad's face hard and very rough
Is it because he's the bravest, and very, very tough?

Why must I learn to write and to read?
I would much rather take my dog for a walk on his lead.
Early to bed then you will grow big and strong.
Why can't parents ever be wrong?

Long walks through woods and meadows green.
The likes of which may never again be seen.
A rabbit's tail disappears down his burrow.
All my yesterdays are gone, there's only the tomorrow.

These are the dreams of my far distant childhood.
I've forgotten the bad ones,
But keep fond memories of the good.

Linda Davies

HOPE

The pain will never come again,
As you have been cured,

Thanks to the medical profession,
Your life has been renewed,

Now you love the spring,
And dew drops on your face,
You're thankful to be alive,
And join the human race.

A holiday in the sun,
As the breeze blows through your hair.

Yes it's you who nearly died,
As they stop to stare.

You glow with laughter,
You're happy now,
With all your loved ones there.

Thank God
Thank God
You sing and dance
With the sunlight in your hair.

Patricia Angus

NICE DAY FOR NICE THOUGHTS!

I am sat in my garden, my dog at my feet
at a round plastic table, on a hard plastic seat.
My mother is knitting, out here in the sun
my husband is walking - his idea of fun!
There are birds all a twitter in the branches above
the fish in my pond . . . I think are in love.
Breezes are blowing straight off the sea
cooling and tanning my mother and me.
Our longest day has been and gone
the weather is kind - so it's summer clothes on.
We've put away woollies, boots and the rest
though my mother, at 86, still needs a vest!
There's tennis on telly for anyone keen
it's Wimbledon here - I never have been.
For a centre court seat I would pay a Kings' ransom
'cos some of those guys are really quite handsome.
We had a visit from Alison just yesterday
our youngest daughter, from miles away.
She brought with her, her son, and her new beau
just for the day - then they all had to go.
Well friend, I've waffled, and this is the end
I just say - take care, and good wishes my friend.
I am sure you will once again drop me a line
till then, adios, adieu, au revoir, and stay fine.

Jenny Payne

A TRAIN'S THOUGHTS

I am a train on a track and I am rumbling by
I go that fast like a blink of an eye.
I whistle and shout with my rolling stock
I know every line on the track.
I have no time to see the scenery
For I have to be on time you see.

It does not matter if I am tired
For I am a train you see.
The driver makes me work at such a speed
He is the one who knows me.
I stop at lights and signals and stations you see.

My driver and me because he and I are a team you see.
We worked together in the cold weather, my poor driver and me.
We go through tracks and cross lines to get people to work on time.

Humans moan and groan if we are not on time, my driver and me.
Workmen on the lines, signals at red, cables on the line, oh what a mess.
Waiting at stations, waiting for signals to go green.

My driver is human you see,
He is a friend, he takes care of me, we are a team.
He knows my moods, I know his, we are good together,
                                        my driver and me.
We slow down to let other trains with their drivers pass.

But humans in the carriages moan and groan, we are doing our best,
Other humans accept that we are doing our best,
I feel my driver smile and say nothing
Because he knows we will soon rest.
Phew

K Horshell

MY BEST FRIEND

Running across the fresh mown lawn
Big black face body fawn
Ears flopping up and down
Not a whimper, not a frown
Tail wagging to and fro
Big brown eyes all aglow
Barking, playing, having fun
Lying rolling in the sun
Chewing on a big brown log
His name is Arnie
He's my dog.

Claire Bloor

PEACE

This great world is a wonderful place
Full of people called the human race
Grandad, nan, father and mother
Aunts and uncles, sisters and brother,
Why can't we all live in peace?

Countries fight one another, it's called war
Don't even know what they're fighting for
Killing and maiming, big and small
Leaving them lying just where they fall
Why can't we all live in peace.

Jungles, they cut down to desolation
To try and build for civilisation
What of the animals? What do they do?
They're just caught and put in a zoo.
Why can't we all live in peace?

The head of the nations get together,
Try to decide as to whether
A disarmament plan would make it cease
Then all the world could live in peace.

J Moorton

Two

No matter where life takes us,
and no matter about the passing of time.
What matters is that you love me,
and that I wished you to be mine.

The two of us have been together,
in almost everything we've ever done.
I've brought smiles of happiness to your face,
while you showed my inner child the beauty of the sun.

I showed you love like no one ever before,
and your eyes told me you appreciated it.
My life may not be forever,
but while it lasts you'll always be a part of it.

When the two of us are together we make life so interesting,
every time I come to yours has been steamy and hot.
When we go out we take our fun with us,
and when parties get boring, then we will follow our own plot.

Honey, these memories I will forever cherish,
from now until the great end begins to start.
Just remember that I'm here for you always
and I love you right until the breaking of my heart.

Darker than the average rose.

Daniel Jones Jr

THE 3 LITTLE PIGS

The 1st little pig built a house of straw,
But the wolf came along and blew down the door.
The 2nd little pig built a house of sticks,
But the wolf was up to his nasty old tricks!
The 3rd little pig built a house of bricks,
But the pigs had a few of their own little tricks -
They built a fire, until it was hot -
The wolf came down the chimney and burnt his bot!
So the moral of the tale is easy but true -
Don't let a bully get the better of you!

L L Holden

MY NIGHT VISITOR

When I was a small child I often used to dream
Of someone reciting, ream after ream,
Of beautiful poetry, before never spoken,
But I could not remember, when I was awoken
The words that in sleep
Struck a chord in me deep.

Pencil and paper I would take up at night,
Hoping to wake up and turn on the light
To capture the words, in my dream softly spoken,
Never at the right time, was my dream ever broken;
This went on for so many years
Through times of joy and times of tears.

I wonder, what was my night visitors' goal
In pouring these words deep into my soul,
Will they remain there, in limbo a while?
Waiting for the day of release, to beguile,
All those whose life may touch mine
Just for a fleeting moment in time.

Jackie S Brooks

THE MERMAID'S LAMENT

Strange sea music whispers in my ear -
The song of the mermaid crystal clear,
Its sadness reached through the midnight air -
A tale of love which none can share.

Her soulful cry tore at my heart -
For she and her lover had to part.
She called to him across the seas,
An echo carried by the breeze.

I knew how she was feeling for
I had suffered like that before.
My own dear love had let me see
That she wished only to be free.

The mermaid called her lover's name
For he had set her heart aflame.
But now she suffered untold pain -
She'd never know such love again.

My heart reached out to bring her peace -
And so, perhaps, my own release!
I'd battle with the mighty wave,
And join her in her ocean grave.

Mary Baird Hammond

UNTITLED

Handsome fly
There was this big fly on the ceiling,
Who had a terrible feeling,
If his wings wouldn't work, he'd look like a berk,
Still handsome but not so appealing.

Fred the spider
I know this smart spider called Fred,
He lives in our old garden shed,
Looking so smart,
There's love in his heart,
Next year he's hoping to wed.

Sea food
This whelk who lived in the sea,
Invited a mussel for tea,
He ate all the food,
I think he was rude,
Just how shellfish one's guest can be?

Betty Hattersley

EX LOVE

I've tried so hard to let you go,
But it's just made me feel low,
All I can think about is you,
I love you so much; I don't know what to do.

I know I said I only wanted to be your friend,
I just want this pain to end,
I want to be by your side,
All the time you are on my mind.

I hate thinking about you with her,
You're with her all the time, it's not fair,
It should be me holding you,
It could have been me.

It is still so hard,
I've still got your Valentine's card,
All you have to do is phone,
And I'll welcome you back into my home.

Claire Murray

NOTHING OR LESS

Artistically paint nothing at all, label, 'abstract,'
Arrant nonsense, unlikely to further contract.
The converse exists, a vague concept of infinity,
A much sought after commodity in this vicinity.

Freely travel the ultimate in pure nothingness,
No colour, insubstantial, wraithlike. More or less,
A celestial black hole, darkness, and hellfire
Retained for that poor metre, to which I aspire.

Journey on, traverse all known galaxies finite,
Through endless space to the sky's outer limit
Pause briefly, wondering, 'How can it be
The only lunatic hereabouts is just me?'

This major opus alas may most probably fail
Through confusion over what serious writing entail.
Doubtless, herefrom, no royalties shall one collect,
Easily double what anyone might dare to expect.

Anne Omnibus

I'M SORRY NOW

I know I sinned, I'm sorry now
I am so sorry I broke my vow.
For I love my God with a fierce strong heart
When I broke my vow we were apart.

Now I cultivate our love again
With a loving beautiful caring chain.
I love you for you forgave me
And gladly I have been set free.

I truly am so sorry now my God
Without your love I did feel odd.
Now I feel you are kind and gentle.
Our love is not fragmental.

Denise Shaw

YOUR MAGIC

When I've had a busy day
When work has been like hell
It's nice to come back home to you
So you can weave your magic spell.

When I walk into the comfort
Of our lovely home
It's nice to have you greet me
To shut out the work place drone.

I love to see your smiling face
The sun's come out again
The dark clouds, they just pass away
Now has gone the pain.

I go and have a shower
To wash away the day
The coldness of the workplace
With the shower fades away.

I dry myself, and have a shave
Get ready for the evening
Then go downstairs to have my meal
This is Heaven, you can believe me.

Here we are, the two of us
Sitting face to face
Your magic spell is working
My heart begins to race.

I wish that I could stay like this
But tomorrow will be the same
It's off to face the world outside
The coldness and the pain.

B Page

MUSICAL REMINDERS
(In Memory of Warren Peacock 1969 - 2003)

Chords that cut like a knife
Remember me so full of life,
The beat thumping on your chest
Think of me at peace, at rest,
When skillfully picked guitar solos scream
See me smiling, living the dream,
So play the tunes we always played
And I'll be up there, on the stage.

A C Small

GOOD DEED

One February when the weather was right
We decided a caravan weekend was in sight
We had a nice time but the weather gave in
My husband said we will go home Cyn
The field was unlevel and the grass had got wet
The wheels they did spin and we got quite upset
An offer of help from a neighbouring couple
He had his arm in a sling but it was quite supple
I took to the wheel and the rest they did push
The caravan moved right out of the slush
Taking it up to the top of the field
I got out real proud, thank yous to yield
Have you ever seen people covered in mud
It's good for a laugh you really should
The wheels of the car had covered them all
White sling as well as I can recall
I said I was sorry but I started giggling
And all the way home with husband and sibling.

Cyn Jordan

I DREAMT OF YOU

I dreamt of you in my sleep
It's something I'll always keep
Tossing and turning
It's keeping me up all night
Hoping and praying that you are alright
I dreamt of your smile
And of your soft gentle touch
Tell me baby do I ask for much?
I hope I have dreams like this forever
And pray to God we'll be together
So sweet dreams my golden child
And may your dreams be worth while!

Anna Yates (17)

TIME

Time is a healer for all things but love,
When your love for him, will always go on,
But after death, forever he is gone.
And time only carves the scars deeper, deeper.
And time only carves the scars deeper.

Time is a healer for all things but death,
When you hear the echoes, of him screaming in pain,
As the anniversary of his death, comes round once again.
And time only carves the scars deeper, deeper.
And time only carves the scars deeper.

Jane Silver

ILL MET BY MOONLIGHT

Above the mountains of Crete the moon is rising in the sky.
Down in the valley, the village sleeps but on a hill a lonely girl cries.
She cries for her love who's gone to sea and she wonders,
If it were he, who's ill met by moonlight.

He'd gone to fish in treacherous waters,
The boy who was her husband to be
When from the village, came that fateful cry,
Ville A Dencia Man amane.
This meant, a ship was lost at sea, now she wonders, if it were he,
Who's ill met by moonlight.

As she lay, so softly, weeping the sound of footsteps she did hear,
And within her heart, she knew, it was the one she loved so dear,
She ran to him, the moon smiled, from above, he'd come back,
Her one true love,
Now they kiss, by moonlight, they kiss by moonlight.

Elizabeth Joyce Walker

TO RUDYARD KIPLING FROM A FEMALE

If you can keep your head, you said,
Wherever your life's path may wind
Untold treasures you will find -
At least, that is how I read!

My dad raised me on your word,
And all my life to date
I have moulded my own fate
On what I read and heard!

I have kept my head and trusted,
I have thought thoughts and dreamed dreams,
And whatever fate befell my schemes
I kept my faith in hope unrusted!

And when dreams dropped in tatters
I have striven with might and main
To build them all up again -
That is what really matters!

But Rudyard, when all is said and done
I think you, and my father, oughta
Know it's harder for a daughter
To be a man, my son!

Dan Pugh

A LITTLE HELP

I help the wife around the house
I help the cat to catch a mouse
I help the dog to catch a rabbit
I help the vicar to change his habit.

I help the tortoise to cross the lawn
I wake the sun when it is dawn
I help the clouds to cross the sky
I help to make the butterfly.

I help the darkness to come to light
I help the moon come out at night
I help the floorboards when they squeak
I help the mountains reach their peak.

I help the fox to be so cunning
I help the tap when it is running
I help the river when it's flowing
I help the plants when they are growing.

I help all things that I can see
I help the leaves stay on the tree
I would have helped the honey bee
But they don't need any help from me.

William G Evans

ONE MAY DAY

I could hear the skylark singing,
Its melody in the valley echoing,
So gently whispered the breeze,
All the blossoms out on the trees,
The year was nineteen-forty-five,
Bees buzzed around the hive,
The war was over it was said,
In the newspaper I had read,
Of all the people that lay dead,
So much sorrow war brings,
I thought as the skylark sings,
I recall a memory of long ago,
My wish was to see war no more,
Over the years wars it has been,
Even more terrible than I had seen,
The future what does it hold?
More wars we are told,
Sadly I end my rhyme,
I have travelled the passage of time,
Nothing has changed, we are at war,
It will be wars for evermore.

Mary Long

FRAMPTON ON SEVERN

An emerald carpet under a blue sky,
That's what Frampton village green was to me.
A piece of old England and that is why
I'll return to that salty estuary.

For two hundred years or more, it's not seen
Plough or feed from man's industrial hand.
In the care of Mother Nature, lush green
As an alpine meadow in distant lands.

On the estuary, wildfowl abound.
Heralds of spring they visit without fail.
In Frampton, lots of songbirds can be found,
If you're patient, you'll hear the nightingale.

The sequoia stands watch over the green,
Reaching out for the sky with its neighbours.
A titan, largest species ever seen,
Alongside elm, oak, lime and black poplar.

You imagine: a misty summer morn,
Jewelled webs strung on the grass for all to see.
The sunshine beaming through the trees at dawn,
The scene - forever in my memory.

Les Davey

Rabbit's Day

Rabbits bounce through the green,
Some are heard and some are seen.
Brothers, sisters, out to eat,
Furry and frisky, light on their feet.
Noise approaches, ears erect,
Burrows close, they all defect.
All is quiet, but still it's green,
Where are the rabbits? None are seen.
Down in the burrow some peep out,
Noise has gone, it was just a rout.

Arthur Williams

CHRISTMAS

N oel, a magical and mystical time of the year.
E choes whisper from forgotten places -
    straining to share their secrets.
W ooded glades, shrouded in a frosty haze.
S tag-headed oaks rise proudly on the skyline,
    stark reminders of winter.
T ales of old whistle through the forest,
    their stories prepared for the ears of the listener.
E vergreens resist the bitter cold as their leaves rustle
    impatiently for the warmth of spring.
A gentle cascade of snow dazzles and shimmers as it tumbles onto
D ark, dampened leaves, cloaking the path that
    will soon receive the tread of St Nicholas . . .

For Christmas has come to *Newstead.*

Matthew Rodger (12)

The Earthworm

The earthworm is a blackbird's favourite food,
A juicy one gives it a great start to the day.
Not everyone likes to see them in the garden,
But gardeners regard them as an indicator of fertility.

Folk like to watch blackbirds after a rain shower,
They also enjoy watching them hunting in the grass.
They do not appear to be concerned for the earthworm,
Anything they do feel will quickly pass.

Of course no one likes to see worm casts on the lawn,
But this is a small price for gardeners to pay.
In producing casts the worms keep the lawn aerated,
The only price we pay is having to sweep them away.

Earthworms are scavengers of leaves and other debris,
Which they eat and discharge as organic matter into the earth,
This keeps the soil nourished and fertile,
A good gardener knows what this is really worth.

The next time you see a blackbird looking for a meal,
Spare a thought for the earthworm whose life will end,
They might not be very attractive in appearance,
But they can be a gardener's best friend.

R Martin

SMOKING

I'm sitting here in the chair
Smoke is billowing everywhere
The ash is long and rather thin
Then I wipe it off my chin

I have a puff now and again
Then a little refrain
The ashtray's full, packed really high
With ash and butts and the occasional fly

I look to the side and what do I see?
A face in the mirror looking back at me
With wrinkles and moles, the hair is thin
Yellowish fingers and nails unclean

The smoke comes out down my noise
Circles around me and then it goes
This can't be me, that, I've seen
The face is drawn, the hair unclean

What is making me look this way?
Is it the puffing and puffing all day
Or is it old age setting in
Making me look drawn and thin?

I'm sure if I stopped, I'd put on weight
And then I'd be a couple of hundredweight
The walls were white but now they're cream
The ceiling is yellow with brown in between

This can't be good, the place looks drab
Is it all because of the fag?

J Eynon

MY DREAM

The perfume of the flowers filled the air
Colours of every hue seemed to be everywhere
The stream that flowed gurgled with delight
All around was such a lovely sight
Butterflies, birds and the bees too
Made up the perfection of this idyllic view
Serene and tranquil with a feeling so rare
It was so quiet and peaceful there
A feeling of stillness and peace inside
Of meeting oneself and the spirit that in us abides
Within each of us upon the Earth
Given to us at the day of our birth
I felt so secure in this wonderful place
Of worry or fear there was no trace
Somehow I knew this was not for real
And I awoke from this glorious dream
Back to my bed and reality
Trying to hold on to the tranquillity
The rare feeling of stillness and peace inside
I will search for each day until the day of my demise
Because in my dream I touched paradise
If I strive hard enough, one day it will be my prize.

Glenys Hannon

THE ENCHANTER

You were my first love
And I remember when we first met
You caressed my body
How could I forget?
Sometimes you were cool,
But still you drew me to you,
I knew I was a fool
But I could not resist
And ran eagerly forward
My body to be kissed!
And your tremendous passion came over me in a wave
For such was your power
And I was your willing slave!
You left my body tingling
And I knew I'd never be free
Ever from temptation
Of my passion for the sea!

June E Howard Elias

HILLTOPS

There is a beauty in Welsh hills
Made green by so much rain,
But riding on a bicycle
Can sometimes be a pain.
Peddling up steep hillsides
Lungs struggling for air,
But when at last we reach the top
Fine views are waiting there.

We stop to get our breath back
While taking in the scene,
The valley down below spread out
A patchwork quilt of green.
When we have rested for a while
From the uphill ride,
Pleasure will replace the pain
As downhill we glide.

Every uphill has its down,
And struggles will all cease
When we reach that hilltop
Where we will rest in peace.

Pamela Evans

LANDFILL

Stormy Down and Nantygywddion are but two of many sites
The cause of public protest and defence of civil rights
Huge depots for the waste of those still living
Running sores on landscapes fair and very unforgiving.

Pristine churches, crumbling chapels mark landfill sites
Where digs and surveys yield delight
About a previous life and its detritus
And is heralded as somehow good for us.

Why is it then that products of our age
In plastic bags committed to the ground
Should be of more concern and rage
Than consumptive cadavers in frail caskets so unsound?

The problem is not new and was foretold
By men of vision and despite the protest remained bold
The answer was cremation and space saving urn
Anathema to some but not those who landfill spurn?

Landfill sites for material of the people by people made redundant
Have outlived a purpose of preserving style and fossilising mystery
Time now for others of knowledge to be bold and not say can't
To combust and sanitise and bequeath a pristine landscape as
                                                    our history.

Mike Hayes

HOPE OF BETTER THINGS

Sunshine fills my window
Sending sun beams above my bed
Will I be here tomorrow or somewhere
Else instead?

Through the night I listen to the
Sounds around about
Sleep, o sleep, where are you?
I will be brave and not call out
It's pain that sleep sin the daytime
At night I fight in vain
Please come soon my daylight
So I can rest again.

I know that I am loved by some people
That is true,
But Lord I need your comfort through
The coming day, please be forever
Near me and never go away.

Now my day is ending
Time's shadows all around
A sense of peace surrounds me
For your great love at last I've found.

Gatekeeper

THAT FIRST KISS

A gentle kiss upon the neck to taste your lover so,
Then slowly around to blushing cheek, all rosy and aglow.
Before the kiss, eyes that close, a wanting look exchanged,
Then lips upon the tearless cheek, once more both hearts engaged.
Slower than those movements now, in time lapse, movements fall,
To join together, by lips alone, then a passionate free for all.
The coming of this sweet embrace, that was so long for yearned,
Gives pleasure, excitement, then lost the time, it was forever spurned,
Then as you draw back, composure find, then that coy furtive glance,
Lips meet yet again in unison, for the lovers to advance.
Now that the scene is set, primed for passions to expand and rise,

The veil of reason falls to hide lovers
From the jealous world's open eyes.

D McDonald

My Advice To You

Give it your best shot,
That's all you can do,
Give it everything you've got,
That's my advice to you.

Go out and beat the rest,
Let your talent shine through,
Prove to the world you're the best,
That's my advice to you.

Not everybody can win,
There has to be losers too,
Never give up, never give in,
That's my advice to you.

Keep coming back for more,
Come back with something special and new,
Keep banging on that door,
That's my advice to you.

You may get there one day.
You may be one of the lucky few,
So don't listen to what people say,
That's my advice to you.

Michael McNulty

MY INARTICULATE HEART

When I speak I always splutter and spout,
My tongue trips and falls over all the words.
I end up sounding foolish and absurd
When I can't get a simple sentence out.

That is the effect this girl has on me,
She makes me become a gibbering fool,
Who can only stand there, stammer and drool
Just besotted by her very beauty.

My heart aches just to pass the time of day,
Hello and small talk about the weather.
But alas I fear that this will never
Occur with self-consciousness in the way.
So each night I lie awake and I dream,
Of tender moments that have never been.

Keith Tissington

A LITTLE DITTY

A little ditty,
Something witty,
I have penned for you,
In rhyming words,
Some quite absurd,
But they will have to do.
I tried all night
To get it right,
Then as the sun arose,
Whilst laid in bed,
I scratched my head
And wriggled all my toes.
I thought I'd found
A rhyming sound,
Poetic phrase, a verse,
Alarm clock rings,
The cockerel sings,
Time to get up, I curse.
I've failed again,
I feel in pain,
No poetry, such sorrow,
But never fear,
Don't shed a tear,
I'll try again tomorrow.

Jim Sargant

WELCOME POETS

I read such lovely poems from people I don't know,
And when I read these poems it's like looking in their soul.

Their thoughts impregnate paper, and saturate with love
I never tire of reading them, seems their words come from above.

Some are about the tragedies they've dealt with in this life
Obstacles they've overcome, when they have had to fight.

The others are amusing, written to make us smile,
We need to see the funny side written in another style.

Everything has opposites, I mean like fat and thin
Good and bad, and then the sad: all battles we can win.

So put your thoughts on paper, deal with them this way
You make some people happy, and troubles sail away.

A variety of happenings greet poets to be sure,
Events come unexpected, they record and make secure.

Poets lonely and depressed will write to pass the time
Through this they find upliftment and maybe peace of mind.

Most poems are a story, how life seems to them,
Written down on paper, is a way of saying, Amen.

Joan Prentice

THE WEDDING

The groom was waiting by the altar rail,
The organist was playing a hymn,
The doors of the church were open,
The congregation were waiting within.

The bride arrived, serene in white,
She was radiant in the warm sunlight,
She looked at her father with a smile,
As in harmony they walked the aisle.

Faces greeted her on either side,
The organist played, *Here Comes The Bride,*
As she neared the alter steps, the groom held out his hand,
And near to her future husband, the lovely bride did stand.

The vicar smiled down upon them and spoke with loving care,
Explaining to them with wisdom the reason they were there,
They made their vows and exchanged rings,
He pronounced them man and wife,
A commitment that they both had made,
Until the end of life.

The vicar gave a final blessing,
For bride and groom to share,
A look of love showed in their eyes
A look that said I care.

And so we wish them happiness,
Blessed by their god above,
What better blessing is there
Than God's own precious love.

I E Percival

A NIP BEFORE BUDDING

It was her first teenage outing;
Outside a tourist office in Fox's Glen
The boys and girls were dancing,
But one girl felt apart. Sal McGinn.

'Sal, enjoy yourself!' called Hannah,
'Shake off your shyness, get a boy,
Don't be choosy; look at my fella.'
Then Bert came over and smiled, *Oh joy!*

Now after all, it was going to be great;
Bert took his camera, put in a film -
He was handsome and walked so straight,
Yes, she felt they could have fun.

Bert said, 'Would you mind moving aside,'
She readily arose and moved her chair -
(He was going to take her photo). 'More this side!
I want to get that girl with the red hair.'

Mary Frances Mooney

THE BIG ISSUE?

Can you see me as you pound your beat?
Can you hear me as you stamp your feet?
Can you really know there's such a one as I?
Do you feel me watching as you eat?
Do you think I like it on the street?
If you do, why don't you break right down and cry?

Did you see the news the other day?
Did you wonder why I lost my way?
Did you ever see me there, but pass me by?
Will you think of me as worthless clay?
Will you scurry home without delay?
While you do, tonight I may lie down and die!

So go wage your wars in lands afar,
Win that oil with which you load your car,
And forget we're here. Just tell yourself the lie
That we like to be the way we are
And we like to sleep under a star.
You can tell yourself all that. You can try!

Marc Rogers

SWALLOWS' DANCE

Dancing in the summer, free, touching Heaven
On telegraph wire, ready to fly by eleven
Motionless in the sky, hovering, catching an insect
Drawn into formation, a leader must be elected.

Now with their heads which seem they are wearing black hoods
Cleaned the victory tails and white waistcoats show their moods
Like aeroplanes they gather their strong groups of newborn broods
Geared up and off they all fly south, past us and to the woods.

An insight or just a calling of nature's command
Ears pick up the thirty-thousand miles radar's band
High in the sky looking down, children are flying a kite
Swallows hope to be overseas, by tomorrow night.

Air currents move us quite swiftly towards the jet stream
Warm and comforting to be floating in the clouds' beams
Landing is still tricky for the young one's but they manoeuvred
Hungry from their flying ordeal, eating cornflowers like a hover.

South Africa is such a long way to journey
Tucked up into a tight little ball of feathers
Dreaming that this would only take till a week on Monday
But as you know this could just be a lot of bleathers.

Well the summertime has been fantastic
Sunny and very hot in gardens, up went umbrellas made of plastic
It's just the job for lazily doing nothing, sweltering and blistering
Beaches are full, sandwiches covered in sand and tempers festering.

Bless this bounty of summer, cheers at Cowan Bay
Waiting, the swallows return back to us by next May
Our gypsy caravan that we had been lended is now being mended
Our greatest thanks to you, the summer, sorry that it has ended.

Jan Ross

THE LINCOLNSHIRE FENS IN MAY

How great to be in Lincolnshire and work outdoors in May
Where you can walk with nature and see wonders every day
The wild duck he has had one clutch and makes his nest again
The moorhen sits upon her nest in sunshine and in rain

The lark is way up in the sky and singing his great tune
He will lay his eggs in the sugarbeet row and hatch them off in June
The wheat fields they are growing well and are almost six inches high
And soon the Harrier will return and plunge down from the sky

He will build his nest down on the ground and then he'll start to mate
He'll then start hunting from dawn till dusk to feed her, she can't wait
The hares they have been chasing around the fields all spring
The little leverets are now running round and will hide under anything

The plover, she has laid her eggs and sits upon the nest
Her mate, he dives down on you if you go near he will protest
The cock pheasant struts around and shows his pride and style
His mate is now so comfortable she has been sitting quite awhile

In three weeks time, she will be proud and strutting with her chicks
May even be a dozen as they start to scratch and pick
You walk along the large drainside and something will catch your eye
It's one of the prettiest sights you're likely to see the kingfisher
                                                            gliding by

He sits upon the dykeside reeds and looks so bright and real
Then you'll see him dive into the stream and come up with a meal
One of the loveliest sights that you might see as the river comes in view
Is a swan sitting on her eggs so proud and graceful too?

But walk too close to the nesting site and you could easily be caught
Her proud male mate is watching you and guards it like a fort
Swooping silently along the dyke banks and hovering once or twice
The barn owl searches high and low hoping to catch some mice

It's great to be in Lincolnshire and see all beautiful things in May
I wish that you could walk with me you would have a lovely day

L Woodhead

MY WISH FOR CHRISTMAS

I've made my wish upon a star that's
travelling to the north,
I hope my baby hears it before
the twenty-fourth.
We've been to lots of parties, he's
stood there very proud,
But I didn't notice, so lost him
in the crowd,
I've been inside a whirlpool and
was too blind to see.
Grant me just this wish so I
can let him know.
That my heart stopped beating,
the day I let him go,
I'll trade in all my presents,
beneath the Christmas tree,
To have my baby by my side,
for all eternity.

Roony

You'd Be So Lovely To Have As A Friend!

You'd be so lovely to have as a friend,
So ready to chat as you are!
I hope that you like all the poems I send!
It's charming to chat up a star!
To me, you look just like a painting
That Renoir would do in his prime!
No wonder the young guys are fainting -
Your gold hair's exquisite, sublime!
Your smiles are like lights in the darkness!
Your laughter sure conquers the gloom!
You're just like a rose grown by Harkness,
Maturing, full beauty in bloom!
Stay pure as a rose made in Heaven
That nothing on Earth can destroy,
As sweet as the cream made in Devon -
For strawberries which we all enjoy!
Beauty's a temporary treasure
As transient as stars up above!
For one's face isn't meant as the measure -
God looks on the heart to find love!
Friendship is just the beginning . . .
The beacon that beckons us near!
Without it, we'd all go on sinning,
With nothing to show but our fear!
That's why I'm so pleased that I've found you!
In essence, your love I commend . . .
Yes, credit where credit is due . . .
You'd be so lovely to have as a friend!

Denis Martindale

ONE TOO MANY

I passed a gypsy in the street,
she caught me by the arm;
She said, 'I've got good news m'dear,
if you'll just cross my palm.'

She said I'd have good health and live
to eighty years or more,
But then through tears she said I'd be
a widow long before.

Now I've been married twice and I'm
resigned to all men's flaws;
I've found that they're of use in spite
of all the grief they cause.

They're good for reaching from high shelves,
they're good for lifting weights,
They keep you warm in bed and this
in some way compensates.

The gypsy said, 'I've more to tell
but it will cost m'dear;
Besides good health you'll have good luck,'
I couldn't wait to hear.

She said, 'Don't think that widowhood
means happiness is through,
You'll marry one more time m'dear
and he will outlive you.'

I grabbed her by her scrawny neck,
I held her by the scruff,
I said, 'You call that fortunate,
my God, aren't two enough?'

Hilary J Cairns

THE WORLD I SEE

Does everyone see such beauty as me?
My eyes are open to the things that I see
A simple shadow or a cloudy day
Is beauty to me in many a way
The rain that falls across my path
Just makes me smile or even laugh

So many places that I've not been
Too much beauty that I've not seen
But every day brings something new
The world is a wonder, I know that's true
So as the sun shines on your face
Sit back and think this world really is a
Beautiful place.

Emma J Riddin

MOLE

Mole's darkened carcass prostrate lay
Upon the grass so green,
His huge hands lifeless as his form
Where once there life had been.

Flies upon his moleskin coat
Laid their eggs at will,
No more he'd leave his telltale heaps
Hill on hill on hill.

No more he'd tunnel by the pond,
By ditch and path and field,
Hunting worms to feed on
In his corridors concealed.

He sleeps now in the arms of time,
Death's torpor on him blessed,
His earthly coat he's hung up
And he's gone to Heaven to rest.

John Wood

BABY

How can anyone harm a defenceless young child?
It's not as if they go really wild!
The moments together are so divine
For a baby that's as cute as mine.

They change your life for better, not for worse,
But some people treat them as if they're a curse.
Turn to this baby when you're feeling down,
And this'll make you smile rather than frown.

The days go by as you watch them grow,
Then one day they'll get up and go.
Make the most of the time you have together,
Because this time won't last forever.

Soon this child will have a life of his own,
Then I will feel like I'm all alone.
Soon one day he will have a family too,
Then there will be grandchildren for me and you.

Jacqueline Appleby

VOTE CATCHING

You really are a naughty boy
as the public you annoy,
The Government with cash in hand
wants you to understand
if you desist in your wrong-doing,
and are no longer ensuing.
They will give you a reward
to stop you from getting bored,
£20,000 is the sum
I'm sure with that you'll have some fun.

So now children at school
who were taught not to break the rule,
find this incentive up their street
so if they lie and steal and cheat,
they'll be given a reward
and none will ever again be ignored.
The Government of course will gloat
as many now for them will vote!

The thought to many will now rise
which is really no surprise,
what of all us aged men
who are three score years and ten?
Not being young, we are forgetful
which I admit, is quite regretful.
So to keep us out of trouble
surely that figure they should double!

D R Thomas

THOSE COLOURS BLUE AND GREY

We snuggled in the cradle,
We held each other's hands
While Ma and Pa watched proudly
And for us did dream their plans.

We slept and dreamt in tandem,
We were brothers of the heart;
We lived carefree in innocence
And we thought we'd never part.

We grew to men together
Then one day you went away
And home life lacked the laughter
Of two brothers at their play.

And my fate too came calling
When I left the family home;
Cruel fate which tempted brothers
To venture all alone.

For then we took up colours,
One was blue and one was grey;
We never knew the sadness
Which was born that fateful day.

And bullets no compassion drew
When we were both mown down
And Ma, she cried a million tears
When we were laid to ground.

Cruel fate which tempted brothers
To the causes of the day;
In the name of freedom lying
'Neath those colours, blue and grey.

Ian C Gray

BOY TO A MAN

Lady when we first met, we connected like
A flock of sheep and we had a child
Together, which made our love for each other
Grow even stronger that it made me feel like
We were inseparable.

As time went by, you began to look more like silver
Than gold in my eyes and the love I had for you
Began to wear off, like the sun without its brightness,

Baby, several months have gone by
And I have had a lot of time to
Think and reminisce about us.

That now I finally realise that you never
Know you have a good thing until it's gone, just like a
Man without a soul or a tree
Without its branches.

Baby the days without your friendship
Felt like morning without sunshine.
An orange without flavour and a rose
Without its scent - lonely!

Lady forgive me for the things I did in the past,
For I was a man with a boy's mentality, like a
Chicken in an egg.

Baby I have finally been through the storm,
The rain, seen grey clouds and blue skies
That it has opened up my eyes and made me
Become a true man.

I am now a working man with a goal to succeed in life.

Baby throughout all the struggles I went through
I realise you are the air that I breath, the sparkle in my soul
And the sunshine on my face.

Baby all I want is your friendship and to be a father
To our child.

Kwaku Emmanual Asafu-Agyei

GOODBYE

I really don't want to leave you this way,
But what can I do, what more can I say?
I know it's hard, so please don't cry,
I'm ready to go, the final goodbye.

It isn't easy for us to part,
I'll carry you always in my heart.
Live life to the full, don't waste time,
It's over for me and you'll be just fine.

I'll miss you so much but not the pain
And I know in my heart that we'll meet again.
Take care my darling, goodbye my love
I'll watch over you from high above.

Susie Field

AS BLIND AS A BAT

I feel so silly for falling in his trap,
I love you baby, now lay on your back.
I thought he was honest, yeah too good for me,
God I was stupid, so blind not to see!
I guess when we're young, we believe what they say,
Think it's romantic in the barn on the hay.
Never listening to Mothers when they say he's not right,
Think *what do they know?* It's me who is bright.
If I had just listened to what Mum had to say,
I wouldn't be pregnant at the end of the day.
Thinking he loved me and with me he would stay,
He said, 'Sorry Baby!' Yeah, just walked away!
Was I really too stupid to see
There was only on thing he wanted from me?
When you think you're ready, make sure he's right,
I'm sorry Mother, I guess I wasn't so bright.

Mandy Jayne Moon

THE CHURCH YIRD-SWINE

A figment of black imagination
Written down in ancient folklore
To frighten village children
With a fate for them in store

Underneath those granite tombstones
Burrowing amongst the dead
Dwelled the loathsome Yird-swine
A myth in yokel's head

Gravedigger always wary
Lest his shovel make contact
With the black and spiny bristles
That would turn a fable fact

Sometimes in still of morning
Subterranean sounds are heard
Perhaps Yird-swine cracking bone
Perhaps village imaginings, absurd

How many coffins plundered
No longer to RIP
When Yird-swine becomes a pig
In its boneyard cemetery

How sweet would taste the bacon
Should Yird-swine 'ere be caught
But we know him only fantasy
So in a butchers, can't be bought

I R Finch

My Christmas Tree

I wish I had a Christmas tree,
I wish I had a family,
For I am so alone.
I walk on by even though I want to cry.

The snow now deep
The cold into my fingers creeps,
And into my tiny feet.
I pass a window,
Into which I take a quiet peep.

A family sit around a Christmas tree,
A family, and I imagine me.
I slowly slide down onto the snow.
My cold now I do not know,
For I am inside. Warmed by my Christmas tree,
And a happy family.

Maria Ann Cahill

ALL OF MY CREATION

I'm going nowhere slowly,
I'm going nowhere fast,
What I need now to help me grow,
Is someone from my past.

A certain man that I adore,
Who gives me inspiration.
He gives me hope and love and faith,
In all of my creation.

Yes, I'm going nowhere slowly
I'm going nowhere fast,
What I need now to help me through
Is love I know will last.

That special man whom I adore,
Who gives me inspiration.
He gives me hope and love and faith
In all of my creation.

Shirley Longford

HELP IS AT HAND

Love of beauty
Love of friends
Feeling so good.
Help is at hand
People's friend,
Space is so infinite,
Twinkling stars,
Echo light.
Spring, summer
Autumn, winter.
Joy, happy party
Under the sky.
Love of life,
A smile and laughter,
Make life worthwhile.

Robert Peckham

PIT AND POT ROT

'How are you? Are you all right?'
'Oh, not too bad - seen better days,
My ankles ache, knees sometimes knock,
Fingers twisted and I can't wind up the clock.

Spine bent double, lungs fit to bust,
Coughing up all night,
But I've been cleared of dust.'

'How am I?
Well I'll tell you in sorrow,
I'm about three weeks better than my mate Fred
And we bury him tomorrow!

I saw him last week,
And he scared me to death.
Three times down the street,
We stopped to take breath.

But he told me last week,
He'd been for his test,
They told him to strip
And sounded his chest.

Start work next week, that's all they said.
Three days later the poor bloke was dead.
Fred never was an idle sod,
But by this time tomorrow
He'll be under the clod.

We used to laugh, him and me,
He said the coal dust I cough up from my lungs,
Would keep your fire going, night and day.
While you, you old bugger
Are only coughing up clay!'

Brian Bateman

FRIENDLY FIRE

A friendly soldier took his life.
We're terribly sorry, they told his wife.
Well, she couldn't hold a grudge for evermore,
So she forgave, these things happen in war.
But why, oh why, did he have to die?
This man who'd beheld her with love in his eye?
Why couldn't it be some other man?
Why had it to be her husband, Dan?

Ian McCrae

To Sarah

Sixteen, a marvellous age to be,
With all life's wonders yet to see.
The world's long journey an open book,
For you to travel and take a look.
Experiences and joy galore
And still there's always room for more.
With open eyes and a searching mind,
You will be amazed what you can find.
Friends you'll make and enemies too,
See that the latter are but few.
A pleasant voyage you can make,
If you learn how to give and take.
So step right in and let's begin
To see the prizes you can win.
The finest thing you'll find in all
Is to hold your head up and walk tall.
For as long as you will have your pride,
You will always feel good inside.
Life's so adventurous at your age,
You only have to turn the page -
And the whole wide world can be your stage.

With all my love, Grandpa.

B Foster

SOMETIMES DREAMS

You wonder where
Your life has been
The unexpected
Sometimes dreams
You never know
What lies ahead
Or where the path
Of life we tread
Will bring such
Wonder and surprise
To brighten up
The darkest skies
A parent brings
Us such delight
Perhaps at first
Some sleepless nights
Though what can bring
Such wonder joy
A house with love
And lots of toys
A brother, sister
Who can share
With Levi
Running up the stairs
A little baby
Warm and sweet
Will make your family
So complete

Jeanette Gaffney

BEAU MY BOA

Gone now the beau that once was my boa,
Snaking about me in the secret of night.
Coiled and curled in our nocturne world,
To awaken at morning in a drowsing delight.
Whatever displeasure I had in some measure,
From cause of ill health or strong will.
The comforting arm worked like a charm,
In the dark, like a cummerbund pill.
That time is the best when the mind is at rest,
Mingling dreams with the comfort of sleep.
Content alike glad sigh as the moon passes by,
With no need for the counting of sheep.
Lying there in the dark we would oft times embark,
Upon some scheme of infinite measure.
But our plans soon were lost in the orbit of cost,
So we settled for our post nuptial pleasure.
A twosome at mind laughter always was kind,
As our story continued to unravel.
Then away went my beau that once was my boa,
When the Chairman knocked down with his gavel.
No use now to pine for what was once mine,
But never will I deign to let go.
Thoughts that one day in love's clandestine way,
I will be coiled in the arm of my boa.

Elwyn Johnson

LETTING YOU GO

I can remember the look in your eyes
There were no tears and no cries
The only way out was to let you go
But that never stopped me loving you so
I said it would not be for long
Oh Pete, how could I be so wrong?

Weekends and holidays, you came home to me
Happiness, it was a joy to see
But when you went back again
Oh my Pete, I ached with pain

I never wanted it this way
For what I have done I will repay
To send away my only son
Was the worst thing I had done

Four years of your life you were away
But now you are back, always to stay.

C Layton

A Glorious Day Of Sunshine

The sun is dawning,
Stretching and yawning,
Embracing the sky
And birds flying by.

Chasing away the night,
With his rays of light.
Dispersing the clouds,
From lingering in crowds.

A blackbird gaily sings,
Whilst preening her wings,
And hers is not a lone voice,
In giving rechoice.

To welcome the day new,
Cows 'bell' and moo,
And sheep offer greetings,
With chorus-like bleatings.

The more he awakes,
Better the day he makes,
By beaming on trees
And warming the breeze.

He kisses the heads
Of flowers in their beds,
Coaxing them to unfurl,
From their slumbering curl.

This golden boy
Fills me with joy,
And I long to absorb
The radiance of the orb.

I'm soon lying outside,
Feeling all sunny inside.
Grateful to have as mine -
A glorious day of sunshine.

Donna June Clift

FORGET-ME-NOT SKIES

A woman so fair
With blonde, sun-streaked hair.
So gracefully slim
With soft, glowing skin.

She shook her proud head;
Full lips looked so red.
A sweet, gentle smile
Played there for a while.

To me, she looked fine
With sensuous line.
Her shiny, blue eyes
Like forget-me-not skies.

Her long, restless stride
Will soon reach my side,
But what could I say
To persuade her to stay.

Her name may be Fay
Or Miranda or Kay.
Such beauty so rare
Has laid my heart bare.

So she was my fate;
I could not escape
A lost dream so fair
With sun in her hair.

If I could just find
This girl in my mind,
IIer shiny, blue eyes
Like forget-me-not skies.

Hazel Mills

DANCE OF THE ABSTRACT WALTZ

Mesmerised by the million cuts it took to form your eyes
Blinded by an innocence that even fools the wise
You move the abstract waltz, trigger lightning bolts that pierce my heart

The fine gold lace that shrouds your face makes my soul
come out and smile
A savoury skin that reveals within, a pureness, the mind of a child
You flow the abstract waltz, show us all our faults, what we are

I watch you play, hear the things you say and reflect on life
You are part of me; I will defend you for eternity with the love I hold
You see the abstract waltz, the key to unlock all my vaults,
leave nowhere to hide.

Child we touch, we embrace, face the challenge that is life,
you are mine
Never will I leave you, forever like the stars above my love, will shine
You are the abstract waltz, far beyond when the heartbeat halts,
the divine.

P Heatley

FORTY TODAY

Your birthday comes just once a year,
But this time you've hit forty.
It's time to let your hair down
And do something really naughty.

You may not be a drinker
But I'm sure that will soon pass,
Cos when you see those wrinkles come
You'll soon be in that glass.

Then aches and pains don't come alone,
Your bum will hit the floor,
Your knockers resting on your knees
And grey hairs by the score.

Forget about those laughter lines,
For they're already set,
A giggle now can cause a fuss,
And get your knickers wet!

I hope this day is special
And have a brilliant time,
And when a stranger asks your age -
Say you're 39!

Belinda Conway

ENDLESS ARMY

Watch now; the endless army
of firmly closed front doors;
gold embossed with
Carinthia, Lime Lodge, Trossach and Elim.
Defended by minimal forecourt ramparts
are these well presented dwellings of small rebellion
convenient to the shops . . .

. . . the little shops that graze contentedly;
dying, being born;
brash bucks and dowdy elders.

And in the night,
the pet mice are not disturbed
by the clicking-clacking shiny heels
of a woman scurrying along the pavement
to safety.

In just one window now
the light is on
as the urban poet writes.

Peter Jones

UNTITLED

You came into the world, eyes wide awake;
You gave your mum, dad and me, quite a shock;
We thought waiting for you, many hours would take,
We were all tensed up, watching the clock.

You arrived to smiles on many happy faces,
Within minutes you had us all under your spell.
You will grow up and visit many new places,
And grow to be . . . ? Well who can tell?

All my love to you Baby,
From Grandma.

Helen Trevatt

MY LOVE FOR THEE

My love for thee transcends all things
I know that it's forever
You're thirty stones - I'm nine stone two
But I will leave you never

The warts don't put me off at all
They emphasise your features
And when you wink, it makes me think
God made some gorgeous creatures!

My darling, when you look at me
My heart beats out of time
When your thyroid's over-active
And your bulging eyes meet mine

Your cellulite's a true delight
Your good leg's got thrombosis
And when I kiss your chaffing lips
The herpes is a bonus!

When bedtime comes and your false teeth
Sit next to your glass eye
I love the way you dribble
As you eat that fourteenth pie

Your wooden leg props up the bed
When you are feeling smutty
I do my best - caress your breast
While you eat a chip butty

So now my love, I hope you'll know
My love for you is utter
True love has seldom been this deep
But that's cos I'm a nutter!

Peter Elliott

THE JOKE'S ON YOU

Happiness is a frame of mind that entertains no sin,
For in a heart that's full of joy it cannot enter in.
Happiness is infectious, try it and you'll see
It will brighten up your day, then you'll agree with me.
My husband's always happy and always writing rhyme,
His name is Eamon Healy, and he's in bed, past nine!
He's called *The Warrior Poet,* Oxford he was born,
He's my loving husband until there's no more dawn.
How about a joke or two, go on crack a smile
Show me your teeth, then you can walk a mile.

Knock! Knock! Who's there? Doctor . . .
Doctor Who? How did you know it was me!
Knock! Knock! Who's there? Boy . . .
Boy who? Little boy blue, not boy who!
Knock! Knock! Who's there? It's I love,
I love who? No it's I love you dear.
You see happiness is only a frame of mind,
Look into your heart - there it you will find.
It's not a bug going around, so smile,
It will brighten your day and all your miles.

It's the sunshine that enters in, so don't dismay,
Smile at someone, go on do it today!
Happiness is infectious, try it, you'll see -
If you've a happy outlook, it rubs off easily.
Tell me a joke, another knock, knock one!
Come on tell me a joke, it will be fun.
Okay. Knock! Knock! Who's there?
Joke! Joke who? The jokes on you.
Now smile and bring some happiness to all people
And shout it to all, at the top of every steeple.

Joyce Healy

CHRISTMAS JOY

Christmas just the thought gives a glow
Love over the centuries each and ever grow
All our loved ones come to mind again
Past and present link in the loving chain

Once again our childhood comes to mind
All the beauty of friends and family find
Today we enjoy what we have together
Happy times, memories, to meet we must endeavour.

Christ, God's Son still has a birthday
All the Christians of the world unite for Bank holiday
Without this break, what a dull, cold time -
No loving meetings or winter break to hear bells chime.

Bessie Groves

KNOCK HARD

Knock hard cos life has left
and more so in the deepest depth
Breathe now cos life is messed
more so in this trivial quest.

Look tough cos life is rough
more so in these times of wrath
. . . Can you remember how to laugh?
Listen to your heart from now
cos life is gonna test you how?
It's gonna throw everything it can at you
while death is on the prowl!

Wave fast cos life is blind, more so
when you are behind
Smile while allowed cos in unison,
life and fear of death
Come to take your last breath.

Live your fun and fire now
cos life will try and put you out.
Don't be a critic cos life ain't that apologetic
more so now
Everybody's a hypocrite that sit and stand . . .
with a gibe in their hand.

Be kind to yourself cos life's an experience
quite hard to accomplish,
Don't take offence just because your life's a mess
you are the insight to yourself.

Shaun Cuthbert

JUSTICE

He tried to kill me and my family
so I killed him back
that's justice!

Don't let some silly ole judge
think otherwise!
I know justice
in the eyes of God.

Hanging's too good
for those swines.
Justice deserves justice
and it's about time
the Courts woke up.

We are far too lenient
with murderers
and it's wrong.
I want justice -
Justice strong.

David Charmen

THE BLUEBELL WOOD
(For all my Hawridge friends)

It was here, in this enchanted place, we paused awhile,
Drowning in the surrounding beauty, the charm and guile
Of a myriad, softly moving, gloriously waving, bluebells,
Breathing in the perfume - laden air of this fairy dell,
And I, transported back in time, to a childhood scene,
Enraptured, as in this idyllic spot, countless blooms did glean,
Yet now I would not harm their grace!

Catch them, while you can, in this merry month of May,
They cannot stay, in glorious array, forever and a day.
Sweet perfection, blooming proudly at the very start,
Their brightness will fade and must very soon depart.
But for now, they proudly show their graceful heads, in unison,
And, as we drink in their beauty, we pause to reason,
That the hand of God is truly here.

We humbly bow, in adoration, for this lowliest of flowers,
Brought to fruition by the timing of April showers.
The colouring of bluebells remains their very own,
There is no other shade to compare, no lovelier tone,
Graciously adorning green swards, under cerulean skies,
There is enchantment here; with bated breath and deep sighs,
We linger, unwilling for the spell to break!

We drank in the sheer perfection of those English woods,
At bluebell time, in delightful May; birds feed tiny broods,
Where the early cuckoo has called, upon his stealthy rounds,
His merry call mingling with rustling woodland sounds,
And we have stayed, luxuriating, under a magic spell.
Our companions to rejoin, reluctant to leave our dell,
Yet anxious to impart our knowledge!

Where sweeps the graceful branches of many varied trees,
The beech still reigns supreme, Queen of all the leas,
And, in this place, in all humility, we bow the knee,
Remarking how closely it resembles a gently-rolling sea,
Doth our bluebell wood, this sunny day, in late spring,
Which we have taken time to explore; our hearts sing,
For we have found contentment here.

Julia Eva Yeardye

FAITHFUL UNTIL THE END
(A tribute to the affectionate fidelity of Greyfriar's Bobby)

He was the pet and watchdog of Constable John Grey.
The tail began when the pup wagged into the policeman's flat.
Hear his son pleading, 'Can we keep him; we have no cat.'

They patrolled the cattle-market soon to start at dawn.
'What an earthy event with buying and selling came Wednesday morn.'
Bobby would scrap with drover's dogs then sniff the straw of the
                                                              livestock.
While his master met old acquaintances and became 'Auld Jock'.

The market finished at midday and so had their beat;
So they sauntered up Candlemaker Row - cobbled and steep
To a tavern where Mrs Ramsay baked pies and boiled stews -
                                                      scalding hot.
Often Bobby was rewarded with a tasty bone from the stewpot.

That 1857 winter was dreich and wet.
After a night's soaking, Jock began suffering the ill effects.
A hacking cough sapped his strength, 'It's murder to breathe!'
Frantically his wife called the doctor, who put him on sick leave.

The withering disease bloodied the blankets like a curse.
'Maybe tomorrow, I'll walk the dog,' but his condition grew worse.
In 1858 Auld Jock died and was buried in Greyfriar's Cemetery.
The mourners noticed the coffin was dogged by an agitated Bobby.

Jock's son carried Bobby home, 'The funeral tea's waiting.'
Refusing to eat, he began to howl as if in mourning.
Mrs Grey unbolted the door, Bobby sped downstairs and up the street.
In the cemetery he found Jock's grave - and curled up and
                                                      went to sleep.

Brown the gardener left food and water beside a gravestone.
A soldier taught Bobby, 'The one o'clock gun means - pal,
                                              here's a bone.'
This famous terrier was painted, written about and gazed at teary-eyed.
On 14th January 1872, Greyfriar's Bobby died.

Fourteen years of hardship and the Edinburgh weather.
- All for the unconditional love of a dog and his master.
Next to Auld Jock the Skye terrier was laid,
Closer than grass and earth on a gravedigger's spade.

Mark Young

WATER TRADER

I am the river, the life giver,
with me you'll never wither.
I am the aviator, the navigator
and compass and key, taking
life to the sea. Stand by me
like a tree or upon me like
an autumn leaf flee.
Rising or falling I'm always
calling, gentle or rough
being plentiful enough.
Frozen yet flowing, still
as the mill but always moving,
replacing and removing, ever
soothing, your destiny choosing.

Vann Scytere

ONE SWEET TOOTH

Saturday's my favourite, there's pocket money due,
Going to the sweet shop to see what else is new.
Bell rings as you enter, eyes light up with glee,
The smell is overwhelming, sweets surrounding me.

Handing me a paper bag, 'Go choose,' she smiled and said
There's sugarcane and sweet white mice hanging overhead.
Jars of coloured candy - red and blue and green,
The biggest chocolate rabbit I have ever seen.

I've nearly filled my bag now, there's plenty more to see,
Piling in the toffee swirls, well maybe two or three.
Raindrop drops, sherbet dip, a lolly on a stick,
Liquorice strips and jelly beans, it could all make you sick.

She wraps the bag so tightly, not leaving any air,
Not tempted even to take one, no I wouldn't dare.
My teeth are all gone now, that is all but the one
Oh, these are not for me, they're for my youngest son.

Teresa Tunaley

EASTERS OF YESTERYEAR

The simple joys of Easter days
When the children all were small.
Were eggs dyed yellow with the *'Whin'* *
That grew beside the wall.

With candle end they wrote their name
(So the dye it wouldn't take).
And when the boiling was all done
Their names stood clear and straight.

They never had much chocolate
For funds were always low.
But Easter when it came around
Had always a special glow.

Sometimes a little fire they'd have
Pretending to camp out.
And toasting bits of bread on twigs
As the dogs sat round about.

The animals joined in everything
And shared the make-believe.
They even pulled a sleigh one day
But *Mush* they didn't heed.

Perhaps our simple Easters
Were nearer God than now
We believed that he had risen
We were rich in Jesus love.
And I think our simple Easters
Were blessed by Him above.

* Local name for gorse bush

Isabel Laffin

DISCIPLE FOR PEACE

Voice heard, come hither lad
Humbly he went
Pathways long, hard
Near a'far
O'er hills, dales, weather cold, inclement.

Solitude
Tranquillity
Quietude
Peace to feel
Beauty of landscape to perceive, greet.

Curlews crying
Wings flapping
Nestlings nigh
Breezes caressing
Waves lapping, rippling o'er golden sands

Soul with pleasure fills
Beholding earth's creation
So he, onward ever to instil
Mankind's mind, words of peace, instruction
Uselessness of war, its devastation, destruction

Neighbourly love, not hate
Inspiring encouraging
Faith, peace of dove
Talks trespasses, forgiving
All sorrows, joys sharing, hopes new, giving.

Ivy Lott

DIZZY DITTIES

'Come into the garden Maud,'
The verger often said,
He tolled the bell,
The congregation to tell,
That the vicar had been there instead.

I went to Sunday School,
In the days of yore,
And my teacher was a platinum blonde.
None of the big boys would pass,
Into the bigger class,
So they found her a place in the choir.

Hey Diddle, Diddle. The Cat And The Fiddle.
You've heard this one before.
At the Women's Total Abstinence Convention,
'Men' you must not mention!
They are all drunken louts and a lot more.

Albert E Bird

WHAT A PONG!

Live in fear is what we do
When he takes off his grimy shoe
What lurks within that man-made shell
Is the most horrific smell

We've used perfumes, deodorants too
Nothing works, what can we do?
They really make us feel so queasy
Cos David's feet are really cheesy

His socks are rotting with the smell
They are the feet that come from Hell
All we can do is just retreat
When David uncovers his smelly feet

Lynn Sheppard

MY SPECIAL TREAT
(To darling Lewis)

Warm soft kisses
peck, peck, peck,
Two little arms around my neck.
It's natures wonder that
you're so small
Can make me feel
ten feet tall.

You have a cute little nose
and sparkling eyes,
Do you know young man,
you are really quite wise?
One look from you and
the world is yours,
Your smile opens up every door.

Jill Perkins

THE MAY QUEENS

We thought that we would stage a Maypole dance display
(after all we were still, just in the month of May)
For our Maypole we found out an old broom handle
No flowers or ribbons . . . just odd strings, a-dangle
Nor did we bother to clean ourselves up that day
as we scruffy kids, set out as Queens of the May
We wandered off around the old lanes in Poole,
This was alright, we were on holiday from school
We found a captive audience of four old men
sitting on a bench, enjoying the sun 'till then
Well, we hopped and skipped and gave them a good show
Puzzled by our antics, they were curious to know
'What be the kids up to today?' One old gent said
As they sat there perplexed, each scratching his head
We had to shout for they were as deaf as could be . . .
So we gave up this idea . . . and went home for tea!

Valerie Ovais

SAVED BY THE BELL

Ring a ding! The school mob's out
Dashing down our street.
Chitter - chatting - this and thating
Busy - bustling feet.

Loitering about in gang loads -
Or shooting down a hill.
It's football on the high roads!
Tea with Uncle Bill.

Soon the hi-fi's blaring -
Mother goes bananas!
Grandpa's started swearing,
He's still in his pyjamas.

'Quieten down at once,' she says
'Grandpa, mind your language.
The kids will soon be on their way,
Then we'll have a sandwich.'

Daphne's in her mini dress,
Ready for a club.
Johnny wants his trousers pressed,
In time for his first job.

'I've only got one pair of hands!'
Mother makes it clear.
'You just don't seem to understand,
When thinking what to wear.'

Monday can't come soon enough,
Mother gives a yell -
The mob go racing down the path,
Ring a ding! It's school!

Wendy Watkin

GONE NOW

Gone now, arms soft and warm
Watery eyes, gentle yet bold.
Gone now, walks in the rain
Shuffling through leaves, red and gold.
Gone now, old hands grasping mine
Whilst paper colours, twisted and twirled
Through the sky.
Gone now, those who loved me,
I cry, I cry!

V I White

THE MASTER ARTIST

High upon the hills' great crest,
There the sun lay down to rest.
Although I am an eternity away,
From this sure wonder, every day.
I surely remember in my thought,
The joy, the sun today has brought.
For as the moon sneaks in for eve,
The magic of creation, I perceive.
It is as if painted with God's hand,
A masterpiece, creation so grand.
It's indeed a wonder, we do desire,
The will to always reach, ever higher.

C R Slater

UNTITLED

A home
Without love
Is merely
A place
Of residence

Brian Thomas

DISTANT HORIZONS

Far off in the distance, past what your eye can see,
there is a place that lingers in your memory,
Beyond that hooded veil of mistiness of sight,
where you can glimpse your true love in that spectral light,
She is waiting for you now, just for the taking,
that somewhere is yours, even when you are waking.

Cut through that uncertainty, let truth search your brain,
Yes! You can see it, let your reasoning sustain.
Allow your thoughts to travel to that place you know,
your life's love is there, it will set your heart aglow.
Yet, it is not of some place but is of a time
when first you met your true love and life was sublime!

You have it still, *there* is no distant horizon,
just a veil in your mind that is your illusion.
Blow it all away then live your life in that love,
reach out with both hands and take this gift from above!

Alan Adcock

MY MARY SO FAIR

She used to be so young and fair
Golden hair was her pride and joy
Full of life and sparkling eyes
When I met her as a boy.

We gathered heather from the hills
The little shamrock from the fields
Danced with our folk until early morn
As they played their favourite reels.

I was a lad in my teens back then
And she was a slip of a lass
We lay in the meadows falling in love
And laughed as we shook off the grass.

We vowed to stay together
For always and forever more
I was so proud of you Mary
With our wedding ring that you wore.

So where are you now Mary?
As I sit here alone to grieve
I'll always, always love you,
Oh Mary, why did you have to leave?

Geraldine McMullan Doherty

BRIGHTER DAYS

You are the sun that's always brightened my day,
You are my rainbow although you stand so far away.
I can see you clearly but I cannot find you,
I've tried a million times but it just won't do.

You are the stars when I look up to the sky,
I'm surrounded by you each and every night.
I fall asleep with the thought of you near,
Then I wake up and realise that you're not here.

I've come to the conclusion that I should just walk away,
Move away from the person whom I live for every day.
It's hard but I'm coping, it shouldn't be too long,
To forget about this love that's still so strong.

Natalie Ellis

ROCK BOTTOM

Rock bottom came knocking hadn't felt it for a while, gave me sadness
I'd tried to forget, that feeling you can't style. Got worried for a
moment captivated by the low, wondered what the point was?
Is it time to go? What good do I do here? What joy have I felt of late?
Just waiting to feel peace, to know that all's okay. To not keep thinking
of others sadness, I can't take away. Why the guilt do I carry?
Why this burden of such shame? Why did I deserve this? What lesson
has manifested again? . . . Numbness -

And then I rise above this, my disdain ebbs away, a moment of light in
my torrid grey day. My confidence collects itself and feeds through the
energy I know, surfing serotonin showing me my way back home, the
connection of my blood lot keeps me on track. I'm prizing out the
positive, the clouds I don't need back. I wonder how I got so low, this
time was the lowest yet. A kick in the arse reminding me that
I shouldn't try to forget . . .

I shouldn't try to cover up the hurt, evaluate my grief. In future I have
to remember - continuation's the only relief.

Kelly Sims

WHERE DOES IT STOP?

There's billions and billions of stars in the sky.
I'm not altogether sure of how or why!
But what puzzles me the most, is where does it end?
Or does it carry on forever in the same trend?
My head's telling me it must stop somewhere.
But if that is so, what would be there?
Most people seem to think there is infinite space
And there couldn't be a different kind of place.
I sometimes picture the universe as a mere marble,
As if to others, it's just significant and small.
But it still doesn't answer the problem I've got,
Because, do their surroundings ever end, or not?
The fact remains that no one knows for sure,
It's not in our power to find out much more.
So, at least no one can argue with what you think or say,
They can't prove you wrong, not yet, anyway.

Justin Stonell

BELIEVE

I believe in miracles,
I believe they come true.
Like when the angels of the heavens,
Guided me to you.

I believe in spirit,
Upon their astral cloud.
I believe the things I've done,
Have often made them proud.

I believe that dreams come true,
When you make a wish so sweet.
I believe that when times are bad,
We all deserve a treat.

I believe there's more to life,
Than growing old.
I believe there's something out there,
Waiting to unfold.

I believe in my children,
Whom I love with all my heart.
I believe that no matter where they are,
We are never far apart.

Donna Salisbury

A GRANDSON

To look on his angelic face
To cuddle him and embrace
A different love I have for him
My heart is full, right to the brim
I feel a bond with him so rare
No other love can yet compare
I love my children, I have four
But I've never felt like this before
Every word he says and games we play
Brings happiness and lights up my day
I'm proud of everything he's done
I'm just crazy about my grandson

Linda Ross

DARLING IT IS AUTUMN NOW

'Mummy where's the birdies gone? I love to see them fly,
I cannot see them in the trees or flying in the sky.'
'Well darling it is autumn now; listen to what I say,
The birdies they don't like the cold, so they have all flown away.'
'Mummy where's the little lambs gone? Those babies you showed me,
What happened to the baby cows? Those ones I loved to see?'
'Well darling it is autumn now; but sweetheart please don't weep,
The cows are all grown up now and the lambs have turned to sheep.'
'Mummy where's the flowers gone? From the garden - Mummy where?
Did they know how much I loved them? Did they know and
did they care?'
'Well darling it is autumn now; please wipe away that tear,
The flowers are all gone away but will be back again next year.'
'Mummy where's the leaves all gone, from the bushes and the trees?
Will all the trees get cold and ill now that they have no leaves?'
'Well darling it is autumn now; the leaves have blown away,
The trees they will not get ill, they'll have leaves another day.'
'Mummy where did the sunshine go? That bright light in the sky?
Why is it going cold now, please Mummy tell me why?'
'Well darling it is autumn now; the sun's on holiday,
It's gone to shine on other children, in countries far away.
But my darling please don't cry because the autumn's here -
The sun will come back, I promise you; it will come back again
next year.'

K Ram

THE GOOD, THE BAD AND THE UGLY

The victims of crime are the ones who are serving time,
They are the ones left to suffer the tragedy
And the criminal is walking free.

Having destroyed not just one life,
But those of others as well,
Condemning them to a living Hell.

The mind recoils at the horrors of humanity,
How can we stamp out this disease contaminating society?

Alongside the good, walks the evil,
The few amongst us - servants of the Devil.
Their minds twisted and corrupted,
The sign of a negative personality,
A person similar in looks to you and me
Being human, yet thinking so differently.

Amongst us there are the good, the bad and the really ugly.
As for the really bad, they'll never change, never reform.
They're no longer human - they can never conform.

The crimes committed are unforgivable,
They have gained nothing but made their own lives unliveable
By their actions - what did they hope to gain
By causing someone great sorrow and pain?

Sheena Razia Qureshi

BABY KNOWS BEST!

I love nothing better than to rest
In that place they call Mum's chest.
For I know I can always rely
On Mum's 'original and best' milk supply!

People keep visiting - one, two now three.
Hoping to catch a glimpse of me,
A gurgle or burp seems to entertain,
Just to oblige - I do it again!

At my cot, they stand and stare,
They don't think I know they're there.
I wonder if they could truly choose,
Would they want me watching them snooze!

I wriggle and squirm in equal measure,
Trying to let them know my displeasure,
They soon realise this means I'm unhappy,
Please, oh please, come change my nappy!

Insisting on dressing me head to toe,
In suits that allow room to grow,
That's why they have an unhealthy need,
To continue giving me too much feed!

So as a form of self-defence,
I am sadly forced to cause offence,
By dribbling and vomiting with some frequency,
That'll teach them to mess with me!

So remember the following . . .

When you're a baby, you cannot comprehend,
How life changes when early years end,
But one thing we certainly cannot deny,
The 'child' within us never passes by!

Selina Duncan

THE LOTTERY

Remember the day you said goodbye,
You said we would never part but that was a lie.
I love someone else, I have done for a while,
'Pack your bags,' you said, 'you're cramping my style.'

You threw me out. On the streets I went,
Just a bag with bits of my life and a bottle of scent.
A place for the homeless is where I reside,
Sick every morning, soon to be with child.

Nature's cruel in every way,
But you know every dog has its day.
There I am walking with my son in town
To buy him night-clothes, like a dressing gown.

A few shops we went in, a great day we had,
Then I saw you begging on the streets, it was sad.
We stood in front of you to see what you've become,
I thought the only thing good you gave me, was your son.

On that day we parted I promised to myself,
No man will ever put me back on the shelf.
You took me for granted, everything I own,
The pain I went through but it's you left alone.

With my dole you spent on drink and gambling,
So I thought to myself, *what's good for him?*
I put a pound on the lottery just for fun,
Guess what? Yes! Isn't it great, *I won!*

Terence Sharon

HARD HAT AND VEST

I am from the North West
Work in a hard hat and vest;
A bricklayer by trade
Use a trowel; hammer and spade.
But a building site is a rough place
When sweat is dripping down your face.
Trying hard to beat the rain
Sometimes seems to be in vain.
If you don't escape the rain
Your effort all goes down the drain!
Mortar gets soaking wet, running everywhere
It's enough to make you despair.
Underfoot it turns to mud
This neither is much good.
There's nothing else to do
But head for the cabin, made of wood,
I would not have it any other way -
For this is how I earn my pay.

S Glover

THE TWISTED FATE OF MANKIND

The world will stand united on a day we'll all remember,
The destruction and devastation on the 11th of September.
Nations torn apart by the tragic loss of lives,
Tormented, tortured people, sent to their graves up in the skies.

Madness caused by people who believe that they're right,
But if they serve their God, surely he doesn't want them to fight.
The oldest story left to man, the one by God we've written,
Gives us hope and courage and something to believe in.

Surely these fanatics can see they don't make sense,
They've twisted their beliefs from what they originally meant.
Which leads us back again to ask the question why?
If we follow our chosen religions, then why must people die?

Lindsay Kelly

My Worst Day

My socks are in a muddle
My pants are really tight
My cat is in the microwave
Giving out a fright.

My mother keeps on singing
I think she needs a pill
She's going to burst my eardrum
Then I'll feel ill.

My breakfast was all burnt
I need a helping hand
My mother put me in a plane
And told me where to land.

I wish I had a sister
She'd be a lot of help
I wouldn't mind a brother
But he'd put me through Hell.

Sophie Mellor (11)

SCRAPHEAP LAMENT

Now just look at me
A boring old bird,
With a middle-aged body
And arteries furred.
An overripe has-been
Who's seen better times!
Would I preserve better
In sunnier climes?

But inside my head
I'm that sexy, young chick,
Who knocked 'em all dead,
Now don't take the mick!
It just goes to show,
That it's never too late.
Don't write me off cos -
I'm past my sell-by date!

Angela Gash

JAMES AND THE SUPERGLUE

Young James had nothing much to do
So tampered with the superglue:
He stuck his brother then aged four
To the teenaged girl next door,
Thus introducing Postman Pat
To hours of endless girlie chat!

He stuck his mother to a gun
(A great big powerful, plastic one).
So when she shopped for frozen peas
The checkout girl fell to her knees,
And shoppers scattered in alarm
While Mother waved her deadly arm.

He stuck his sister to a chair;
He glued his grandad to the stairs;
He stuck the house keys in their locks,
And glued Gran's chocolates in their box.
James laughed with glee at all these tricks
Then sabotaged the Lego bricks.

Disaster struck with dreadful ease:
James glued his elbow to his knees.
In struggling to escape the glue
He fixed his fingers to his shoe;
Then fell, and with a final squirt
He stuck his forehead to his shirt!

Young James lay struggling on the ground,
And hours elapsed before they found
Him writhing in a painful knot,
And Father said, 'You should be shot!'
While Mother did not even speak,
But left him there another week . . .

Tim Harvey

IF I COULD LIVE MY LIFE AGAIN

If I could live my life again, what age would I be?
A sweet young bride, a teenager, a babe on mother's knee!

Perhaps I would choose to be a babe, to be safe, snug and warm,
loving arms to hold me tight and keep me free from harm.

Would I be a teenager, dancing the night away, with lips so bright,
hair piled high, hips that always sway?

Maybe to be a bride again, with dress and veil so white.
Different arms to keep me safe and hold me through the night.

What about the time I had my lovely family, wakeful nights,
chubby hands and arms outstretched to me.

A time I would not choose again, a pain so hard to bear,
was when I lost the one I loved, his strength no longer there.

The time I would have to choose, would have to be today,
my grandchildren make my life worthwhile,
so I'll enjoy them while I may.

Elizabeth Walton

THE STORM

The storm it raged. The sky was black and low,
The little ship, she fought tremendous seas.
The north east wind, its hardest, it did blow.
Would the storms great fury ever cease?
They pitched and rolled, it looked like annihilation.
The wind it shrieked through halyards drenched in spray,
But every man stood steadfast at his station.
For the safety of their ship, they all did pray.
God keep her safe from the element's vile temper,
Help us with Thy goodness on our way,
And with the guiding light that you have sent us,
We will see the dawning of a brighter day.

C Wilkinson

SMILE A SMILE

Smile a smile
Do not frown
Even though you're feeling down

Laugh a laugh
Call a friend
Someone on whom you can depend

Life is short
There's not much time
Don't waste it all, it will be fine

Grab each day
Love a lot
Make the most of what you've got

As all too soon
You will age
And your life turns another page

Keep looking good
Dress to kill
Whatever age, love yourself still

If you're feeling rather sad
Stay looking happy
And think of things that makes you glad

After all, life's a journey
Make it great
Of this you're worthy

So don't waste a single minute
Life's so precious
Get out there
Live it!

Tricia Cervasio

A Tale Of Long Ago

My love's face, so pale in the soft moonlight
And her eyes were full of silver starlight.
Her hair gleamed dark as a raven's wing;
As many melodious songs she'd sing

Of times long past and stories untold;
Brave knights on chargers in cloth of gold;
Maidens rescued from terrible plights
And kings locked into their deadly fights.

She rests in a bower of roses white
And, shares her thoughts 'neath a moonlit night.
The perfume of flowers hangs in the air
Around my love with the raven hair.

My love lives in the time of long ago
And the years have become my darkest foe.
I reach out to her through the mists of time,
So sure in my heart she can never be mine.

Hazel Mills

THE EYE IN THE SKY

It rotates around from top to bottom,
Carrying its vessels way up high.
Revolving around from its fixed position,
The eye in the sky.

Bring your friends, your relatives,
Tell them to go and they'll comply.
Revolving around from its fixed position,
The eye in the sky.

Millions queue up to take a ride,
Over the whole of London you can cast an eye.
Revolving around from its fixed position,
The eye in the sky.

Once you're on, you don't want to stop,
From the top everyone looks like a small fry.
Revolving around from its fixed position,
The eye in the sky.

See the sights, see Big Ben,
From your vessel way up high.
Revolving around from its fixed position,
The eye in the sky.

Mrinalini Dey

A FRIEND OF SOCRATES

A crafted head details lean visage, in clay,
Once fired to cinnamon hue.
The provenance, Oran, a magic display,
White houses and marble and blue.

A curly haired youth with eyes blank in a stare,
A royal or stoical pose.
Perhaps a slave, in a lair he would forswear,
And blind after all, no one knows.

A decapitation, a cut thorough neck,
Agility maimed by events.
Horizon's hope, momentary, just a speck,
Grabbed by political currents.

The wind at Djemila turned northern that night,
With Roman armed conquest and force.
Those captured were butchered and tarred at first light,
Atonement for their gods, remorse.

The citizens calm, under Rome Rule again,
The foreign wars gut the poor homes.
The secret societies lift the young men,
Djemila's winds haunt catacombs.

A clay figurine is exposed in the sand,
Tossing in Djemila's dank breeze.
A great old philosopher takes it in hand,
Allows it to flee Little-Ease.

Anthony M Blackwell

CHURCH PICNIC

The haze and blaze of sunlight hues
    carpet of dry grass, no morning dews
Blankets lay strewn, image of modern art
    A guzzle of picnic delicacies, a lá cartè
indulgence for any eclectic palate
    oyster salad, tofu hard as sallet
a display of continental cheeses and bread
    succulent fruit from far as the Med
An assortment of young and old
    hands reach into the platters bold
eager to quench their hunger pang
    church picnic with a bang.

Catherine Mark

WHAT WOULD YOU SAY?

If I showed you my wildest dreams
Would you look at me and sigh?
If I showed my haunting nightmares
Would you look at me and cry?

If I shared my sacred secrets
Would you promise to never tell?
If I let you walk in my shoes
Would you lead me into Hell?

When I came into your dream that night
Did you look at me in fear?
When I took away your haunting nightmares
Did you look at me and cheer?

When you told me all your secrets
Did you think I would tell anyone?
When I walked the path you walked before
Did you think I'd lead you wrong?

Peter Wesley Hayward

CHIVALRY

At bus or train or underground,
This type of man is easily found,
Umbrella, briefcase, pin-striped suit,
Brylcreemed hair, polished boots.
Underarm, his paper stored,
When transport comes, he's first aboard.
Sits down, spreads his broadsheet wide,
Behind the headlines, his face, he hides.
Ignoring all around him, standing,
No eye contact made, just pages turning.
Standing then, he turns and smiles,
At pregnant woman in the aisle,
'Madam please do have my seat,
Sit down here, rest your feet.'
Belongings gathered, out he hops
Not chivalrous really, it was his stop!

Frances Ridett

TIMES LIFE

One x two
A blue, shiny shoe

Two x three
A widow's plea

Three x four
Feel the rain pour

Four x five
An African deprived

Five x six
Take your pick

Six x seven
Hell or Heaven

Seven x eight
Your life laid on a plate

Eight x nine
Repulsive or divine

Nine x ten
We start again

Melanie Rowe

THOUGHTS OF HOME

An old man dreaming in the sun
    lost in the past
When his young life had scarce begun
    in Ireland's green and quiet land.

Not for him the stealthy creeping out at night
    the whispering password
No bombs shattered his life
    or gave him cause to hide.

In the Ireland he remembers, days of long ago
Working in the fields, the stony fields
    that still gave food for life
A simple life of work and home
    and peaceful nights.

Oh that Ireland now could
    be like this man's dream
That peace could once again become reality
    and Ireland be united once again.

Mary O'Connell

ETERNITY

The time has come for me to go
but please don't feel low,
For I will be waiting somewhere above
for my one and only love.
So don't you rush on my account
you live a full and happy life
and don't forget my dearest love
we belong together like turtle doves.
As for now, I will sit and wait
until we meet at them pearly gates.
Please don't be sad or blue
just remember . . . I love you.

Tracey Stanton

SELF-CONFIDENCE

It's a mysterious force
So let nature take its course
There is nothing new about the theme
It's confidence of course
Confidence
Just confidence

It will help you up a slope
Just you cling on to that rope
And reach deeper in yourself
When you feel you cannot cope
For confidence, more confidence

So if a mountain or a hill
Pose a challenge for you still
The answer to that question
Lies in the belief that you will
With confidence
Self-confidence.

High Priest

FAMILY DO'S

The thing I hate about barbecues
Or other special family do's,
Is when they die off at the end
And it's 'bye-bye' to family and friends.
I feel deserted and alone
Even with my family who live at home.
Why can't these things last forever,
When everyone's happy, spending time together?

Stephanie Cox

ANTISOCIAL BEHAVIOUR

WKD bottles smashed,
Blue beer cans squashed and strewn;
Debris from the partying
Beneath this weekend's moon

Music booming from the cars
Of silver, black and red,
Driving all the neighbourhood,
Sleep deprived, from bed

Intimidating passers-by,
Abuse and laughter thrown,
As drugs and solvents give these youths
What courage they have shown

Handbrake turns and hooting horns
To loud applause and yells;
Those antisocial antics
Only dawn's arrival quells.

Kim Montia

DUST TO DUST

A stillness fills the midnight air,
  Echoes surrounds us unaware.
    Momentarily a chill cascades
      Our persona like a shadow,
        Imagining the fine dust turning into matter.

Soon like so many in this endless sleep,
  We will return to our true spirit.
    Having relived a thousand karma's.
      Our soul to rest in peace at last.
        All pain and suffering replaced by eternal happiness.

Catherine Keepin

A FRIEND IN ME

Are the notes of birdsong,
The raven enjoys to sing,
As full of doom and gloom
Like that he's meant to bring?

Is he really the black demon
He's reputedly said to be?
Or is he just misunderstood
And hoping, someday, I'll see?

Do his ever-watchful eyes
Survey all for the Devil below.
Or is he simply catching mine,
To see if I already do know?

From that day, my life changed,
Because of a series of dreams,
For I began to slowly hear
A melody to his screams.

The misconceptions that I had,
Have been rectified at last
And the fear I had of him,
Is now lost in the past.

I've seen his initial self,
As sent from Heaven above.
When he was feathered white,
And bore love akin the dove.

He just wanted a friend
And hoped that friend was me,
Which he asked with a tune,
But his tune was out of key!

I am thankful for the day
Our friendship first occurred.
For he is not an evil omen,
But in fact, a lucky bird!

Donna June Clift

BITTER CONSCIENCE

Twilight brings its bitter taste back to me
And loneliness has filled me with despair
I wonder if I'll find a place to be
I'll take a risk and gamble on a dare.
The raven sings to me its lullaby
But I have no candle to light the way
Sometimes I wish to shrivel up and die
I'm not going to, at least not this day.
The dawn gives to me a little more hope
And Friday's angel grants me little grace
I now refuse to sit around and mope
And a little smile creeps across my face.
I know I'll make it through the path of life
And Death will not yet claim me with his scythe.

Daniel Dyson (14)

FLY

I want to fly, fly high, fly far away,
Away from this cold darkened day.
I want to fly through the night,
Spread my wings and take flight.
Higher than Heaven, how far is space?
To just go, leave without a trace.
Kiss the stars, to embrace the moon,
Not much longer, I'll be there soon.
To grasp Saturn within my arms,
Dance away with all its charms.

I want to fly, fly high, fly far away . . .

Nikohl Medley

RURAL HARMONY

I love the sound of robins and rooks
And whispering trees and crickets;
Of owls at night and swans in flight
And running things through thickets.

Humming bees, a foxes bark
Sparrows all debating.
The distant bleat of one lost sheep
For me is quite elating;
Raucous geese and chirping finch,
Moles that burrow inch by inch.
Their is a harmony of sound
Hearing nature in the round.

The blend of creatures great and small
In their rural music hall!

Cyril Joyce

THANK YOU TOO

My friend,
Whenever I was blue,
There was you,
You held me up,
That's what friends do,
So I am saying,
Thank you,
You helped me so much,
I just can't tell how
I needed you too,
When I was feeling so blue,
I cannot write songs like you do,
So this poem is for you,
And Emma -
Thank you for being a friend,
Because you cared about me too.

Pauline Lamont

I Remember It well

Now hear me Son, I have something to say
When I was young, I thought that way
When I was sixteen, I was hard to please
But my mother pleaded on bended knees
And my father said, 'Son you listen to me,'
But I was much too headstrong to see
He said, 'My way is the way things are done
This is the way my house is run
I know you're sixteen and you want fun
But it's my duty to guide you, Son
It's just not on to talk that way
Now keep quiet, if you want to stay.'
Then I said, 'No, not any more,'
As I bolted through the door.

Years came and went and then one day
I was coming back to say
To say I was sorry, I was back at the door
And I wouldn't do it any more
I no longer want to be me
I want to be part of my family
But the house was deserted
My parents had died
Oh how sorry I was, oh, the tears I cried
One day I was young, just like you
I remember it well, I was sixteen too

Joan Magennis

HIDDEN HOLLOW

Remember a breeze who no longer blows,
recall a river that forever flows
by way of a forest, which gratefully grows
unchecked upon a spring's secret hollow,
where dryads dwell with fawns who follow
a sound singing an awakened lament,
to a woodland home aptly spent,
straddling a glen beneath rugged braes,
obscured from view by Sol's seasonal haze.
Overlooked oaks enclose beechen vale,
encircling our valley, esoteric dale,
Affadil, primrose, sorrel slipped bells,
senses engulfed with wonderful smells,
echoes resound creating sonorous melodies,
resonating fully through harmonious trees,
returned to the fore, her forgotten breeze.

Drew Hawfawn

FRIENDSHIP

True friendship warm and all sincere,
Holds a glow that's very dear.
This something money cannot buy,
Will help to guide us till we die.
When times are hard and days are bleak,
The company of friends we seek . . .
To know when trouble's piling high
A should dear on which to cry.
Far better trusted friendships few
Than hundreds that are not so true.

Pearl M Burdock

JUDGEMENT DAY

Old man rocks and reminisces
Of old times blurred around the edges.
Tired old mind proves a conspiring companion
Forgetting the laden ghostly galleon
Full sail of his evil and murderous thoughts
Fleetingly out of shadows brought,
Now lost in memory's darkest cavern.

Old man hums a nursery rhyme
Remembered from an innocent time.
Forgotten is the half-turned face
Eyes staring from a life's tortured waste.

His own reflection he refuses to see
Only his smile which promises to please -
But it is the smile of deception
Before the kiss of death
Which cuckolds the old man
When he draws his last breaths
As one by one, silently filing by,
Is every heinous deed he sought to deny.

P Carleton

LOST LOVED ONES

You came into our life
Like the sun into the dark.
'Tis a shame you left us
Our paths, they had to part.

Now you are in Heaven
But always in our hearts,
We think of you each morning
Before our day does start.

A child is a treasure
An adult a gem
Even when they are gone
Your heart remembers them.

Carl Spencer